Betty Kirsch

WINTERSET

WINTERSET

A PLAY IN THREE ACTS

BY

Maxwell Anderson

PUBLISHED BY

ANDERSON HOUSE

WASHINGTON

1935

NOTE

GEORGE BANTA PUBLISHING COMPANY, MENASHA, WISCONSIN

CHARACTERS

TROCK
SHADOW
GARTH
MIRIAMNE
ESDRAS
THE HOBO
1ST GIRL
2ND GIRL
JUDGE GAUNT
MIO
CARR
HERMAN
LUCIA
PINY
A SAILOR
STREET URCHIN
POLICEMAN
RADICAL
SERGEANT
Non-speaking
URCHINS
TWO MEN IN BLUE SERGE

WINTERSET
ACT ONE

ACT ONE

SCENE I

SCENE: *The scene is the bank of a river under a bridgehead. A gigantic span starts from the rear of the stage and appears to lift over the heads of the audience and out to the left. At the right rear is a wall of solid supporting masonry. To the left an apartment building abuts against the bridge and forms the left wall of the stage with a dark basement window and a door in the brick wall. To the right, and in the foreground, an outcropping of original rock makes a barricade behind which one may enter through a cleft. To the rear, against the masonry, two sheds have been built by waifs and strays for shelter. The river bank, in the foreground, is black rock worn smooth by years of trampling. There is room for exit and entrance to the left around the apartment house, also around the rock to the right. A single street lamp is seen at the left—and a glimmer of apartment lights in the background beyond. It is an early, dark December morning.*

TWO YOUNG MEN IN SERGE *lean against the masonry, matching bills.* TROCK ESTRELLA *and* SHADOW *come in from the left.*

Trock. Go back and watch the car.

[*The* TWO YOUNG MEN *go out.* TROCK *walks to the corner and looks toward the city*]

You roost of punks and gulls! Sleep, sleep it off,
whatever you had last night, get down in warm,
one big ham-fat against another—sleep,
cling, sleep and rot! Rot out your pasty guts
with diddling, you had no brain to begin. If you had
there'd be no need for us to sleep on iron
who had too much brains for you.

Shadow. Now look, Trock, look,
  what would the warden say to talk like that?

Trock. May they die as I die!
  By God, what life they've left me
  they shall keep me well! I'll have that out of them—
  these pismires that walk like men!

Shadow. Because, look, chief,
  it's all against science and penology
  for you to get out and begin to cuss that way
  before your prison vittles are out of you. Hell,
  you're supposed to leave the pen full of high thought,
  kind of noble-like, loving toward all mankind,
  ready to kiss their feet—or whatever parts
  they stick out toward you. Look at me!

Trock. I see you.
  And even you may not live as long as you think.
  You think too many things are funny. Well, laugh.
  But it's not so funny.

Shadow. Come on, Trock, you know me.
  Anything you say goes, but give me leave
  to kid a little.

Trock. Then laugh at somebody else!
  It's a lot safer! They've soaked me once too often
  in that vat of poisoned hell they keep up-state
  to soak men in, and I'm rotten inside, I'm all
  one liquid puke inside where I had lungs
  once, like yourself! And now they want to get me
  and stir me in again—and that'd kill me—

and that's fine for them. But before that happens to me
a lot of these healthy boys'll know what it's like
when you try to breathe and have no place to put air—
they'll learn it from me!

Shadow. They've got nothing on you, chief.

Trock. I don't know yet. That's what I'm here to find out.
If they've got what they might have
it's not a year this time—
no, nor ten. It's screwed down under a lid.—
I can die quick enough, without help.

Shadow. You're the skinny kind
that lives forever.

Trock. He gave me a half a year,
the doc at the gate.

Shadow. Jesus.

Trock. Six months I get,
and the rest's dirt, six feet.

> [LUCIA, *the street-piano man, comes in right from behind the
> rock and goes to the shed where he keeps his piano.*
> PINY, *the apple-woman, follows and stands in the en-
> trance.* LUCIA *speaks to Estrella, who still stands facing
> Shadow*]

Lucia. Morning.

> [TROCK *and* SHADOW *go out round the apartment house without
> speaking*]

Piny. Now what would you call them?

Lucia. Maybe someting da river washed up.

Piny. Nothing ever washed him—that black one.

Lucia. Maybe not, maybe so. More like his pa and ma raise-a heem in da cellar.

[*He wheels out the piano*]

Piny. He certainly gave me a turn.

[*She lays a hand on the rock*]

Lucia. You don' live-a right, ol' gal. Take heem easy. Look on da bright-a side. Never say-a die. Me, every day in every way I getta be da regular heller.

[*He starts out*]

CURTAIN

ACT ONE
Scene II

Scene: *A cellar apartment under the apartment building, floored with cement and roofed with huge boa constrictor pipes that run slantwise from left to right, dwarfing the room. An outside door opens to the left and a door at the right rear leads to the interior of the place. A low squat window to the left. A table at the rear and a few chairs and books make up the furniture.* Garth, *son of Esdras, sits alone, holding a violin upside down to inspect a crack at its base. He lays the bow on the floor and runs his fingers over the joint.* Miriamne *enters from the rear, a girl of fifteen.* Garth *looks up, then down again.*

Miriamne. Garth—

Garth. The glue lets go. It's the steam, I guess.
  It splits the hair on your head.

Miriamne. It can't be mended?

Garth. I can't mend it.
  No doubt there are fellows somewhere
  who'd mend it for a dollar—and glad to do it.
  That is if I had a dollar.—Got a dollar?
  No, I thought not.

Miriamne. Garth, you've sat at home here
  three days now. You haven't gone out at all.
  Something frightens you.

Garth. Yes?

Miriamne. And father's frightened.
  He reads without knowing where. When a shadow falls

7

across the page he waits for a blow to follow
after the shadow. Then in a little while
he puts his book down softly and goes out
to see who passed.

Garth.   A bill collector, maybe.
We haven't paid the rent.

Miriamne. No.

Garth. You're a bright girl, sis.—
You see too much. You run along and cook.
Why don't you go to school?

Miriamne. I don't like school.
They whisper behind my back.

Garth. Yes? About what?

Miriamne. What did the lawyer mean
that wrote to you?

Garth.

   [*Rising*]

What lawyer?

Miriamne. I found a letter
on the floor of your room. He said, "Don't get me wrong,
but stay in out of the rain the next few days,
just for instance."

Garth. I thought I burned that letter.

Miriamne. Afterward you did. And then what was printed
about the Estrella gang—you hid it from me,
you and father. What is it—about this murder—?

Garth. Will you shut up, you fool!

Miriamne. But if you know
why don't you tell them, Garth?
If it's true—what they say—
you knew all the time Romagna wasn't guilty,
and could have said so—

Garth. Everybody knew
Romagna wasn't guilty! But they weren't listening
to evidence in his favor. They didn't want it.
They don't want it now.

Miriamne. But was that why
they never called on you?—

Garth. So far as I know
they never'd heard of me—and I can assure you
I knew nothing about it—

Miriamne. But something's wrong—
and it worries father—

Garth. What could be wrong?

Miriamne. I don't know.

    [*A pause*]

Garth. And I don't know. You're a good kid, Miriamne,
but you see too many movies. I wasn't mixed up
in any murder, and I don't mean to be.
If I had a dollar to get my fiddle fixed
and another to hire a hall, by God I'd fiddle
some of the prodigies back into Sunday School
where they belong, but I won't get either, and so

I sit here and bite my nails—but if you hoped
I had some criminal romantic past
you'll have to look again!

Miriamne. Oh, Garth, forgive me—
But I want you to be so far above such things
nothing could frighten you. When you seem to shrink
and be afraid, and you're the brother I love,
I want to run there and cry, if there's any question
they care to ask, you'll be quick and glad to answer,
for there's nothing to conceal!

Garth. And that's all true—

Miriamne. But then I remember—
how you dim the lights—
and we go early to bed—and speak in whispers—
and I could think there's a death somewhere behind us—
an evil death—

Garth.

[*Hearing a step*]

Now for God's sake, be quiet!

[ESDRAS, *an old rabbi with a kindly face, enters from the outside. He is hurried and troubled*]

Esdras. I wish to speak alone with someone here
if I may have this room. Miriamne—

Miriamne.

[*Turning to go*]

Yes, father.

[*The outer door is suddenly thrown open.* TROCK *appears*]

Trock.

[*After a pause*]

You'll excuse me for not knocking.

[SHADOW *follows Trock in*]

Sometimes it's best to come in quiet. Sometimes
it's a good way to go out. Garth's home, I see.
He might not have been here if I made a point
of knocking at doors.

Garth. How are you, Trock?

Trock. I guess
you can see how I am.

[*To Miriamne*]

Stay here. Stay where you are.
We'd like to make your acquaintance.
—If you want the facts
I'm no better than usual, thanks. Not enough sun,
my physician tells me. Too much close confinement.
A lack of exercise and an overplus
of beans in the diet. You've done well, no doubt?

Garth. I don't know what makes you think so.

Trock. Who's the family?

Garth. My father and my sister.

Trock. Happy to meet you.
Step inside a minute. The boy and I
have something to talk about.

Esdras. No, no—he's said nothing—
nothing, sir, nothing!

Trock. When I say go out, you go—

Esdras.

[*Pointing to the door*]

Miriamne—

Garth. Go on out, both of you!

Esdras. Oh, sir—I'm old—
old and unhappy—

Garth. Go on!

[Miriamne *and* Esdras *go inside*]

Trock. And if you listen
I'll riddle that door!

[Shadow *shuts the door behind them and stands against it*]

I just got out, you see,
and I pay my first call on you.

Garth. Maybe you think
I'm not in the same jam you are.

Trock. That's what I do think.
Who started looking this up?

Garth. I wish I knew,
and I wish he was in hell! Some damned professor
with nothing else to do. If you saw his stuff
you know as much as I do.

Trock. It wasn't you
turning state's evidence?

Garth. Hell, Trock, use your brain!
   The case was closed. They burned Romagna for it
   and that finished it. Why should I look for trouble
   and maybe get burned myself?

Trock. Boy, I don't know,
   but I just thought I'd find out.

Garth. I'm going straight, Trock.
   I can play this thing, and I'm trying to make a living.
   I haven't talked and nobody's talked to me.
   Christ—it's the last thing I'd want!

Trock. Your old man knows.

Garth. That's where I got the money that last time
   when you needed it. He had a little saved up,
   but I had to tell him to get it. He's as safe
   as Shadow there.

Trock.

   [*Looking at Shadow*]

   There could be people safer
   than that son-of-a-bitch.

Shadow. Who?

Trock. You'd be safer dead
   along with some other gorillas.

Shadow. It's beginning to look
   as if you'd feel safer with everybody dead,
   the whole god-damn world.

Trock. I would. These Jesus-bitten
    professors! Looking up their half-ass cases!
    We've got enough without that.

Garth. There's no evidence
    to reopen the thing.

Trock. And suppose they called on you
    and asked you to testify?

Garth. Why then I'd tell 'em
    that all I know is what I read in the papers.
    And I'd stick to that.

Trock. How much does your sister know?

Garth. I'm honest with you, Trock. She read my name
    in the professor's pamphlet, and she was scared
    the way anybody would be. She got nothing
    from me, and anyway she'd go to the chair
    herself before she'd send me there.

Trock. Like hell.

Garth. Besides, who wants to go to trial again
    except the radicals?—You and I won't spill
    and unless we did there's nothing to take to court
    as far as I know. Let the radicals go on howling
    about getting a dirty deal. They always howl
    and nobody gives a damn. This professor's red—
    everybody knows it.

Trock. You're forgetting the judge.
    Where's the damn judge?

Garth. What judge?

Trock. Read the morning papers.
It says Judge Gaunt's gone off his nut. He's got
that damn trial on his mind, and been going round
proving to everybody he was right all the time
and the radicals were guilty—stopping people
in the street to prove it—and now he's nuts entirely
and nobody knows where he is.

Garth. Why don't they know?

Trock. Because he's on the loose somewhere! They've got
the police of three cities looking for him.

Garth. Judge Gaunt?

Trock. Yes. Judge Gaunt.

Shadow. Why should that worry you?
He's crazy, ain't he? And even if he wasn't
he's arguing on your side. You're jittery, chief.
God, all the judges are looney. You've got the jitters,
and you'll damn well give yourself away some time
peeing yourself in public.

[TROCK *half turns toward Shadow in anger*]

Don't jump the gun now,
I've got pockets in my clothes, too.

[*His hand is in his coat pocket*]

Trock. All right. Take it easy.

[*He takes his hand from his pocket, and* SHADOW *does the same*]
[*To Garth*]

Maybe you're lying to me and maybe you're not.
Stay at home a few days.

Garth. Sure thing. Why not?

Trock. And when I say stay home I mean stay home.
If I have to go looking for you you'll stay a long time
wherever I find you.

[*To Shadow*]

Come on. We'll get out of here.

[*To Garth*]

Be seeing you.

[SHADOW *and* TROCK *go out. After a pause* GARTH *walks over
to his chair and picks up the violin. Then he puts it
down and goes to the inside door, which he opens*]

Garth. He's gone.

[MIRIAMNE *enters,* ESDRAS *behind her*]

Miriamne.

[*Going up to Garth*]

Let's not stay here.

[*She puts her hands on his arms*]

I thought he'd come for something—horrible.
Is he coming back?

Garth. I don't know.

Miriamne. Who is he, Garth?

Garth. He'd kill me if I told you who he is,
that is, if he knew.

Miriamne. Then don't say it—

Garth. Yes, and I'll say it! I was with a gang one time
that robbed a pay roll. I saw a murder done,
and Trock Estrella did it. If that got out
I'd go to the chair and so would he—that's why
he was here today—

Miriamne. But that's not true—

Esdras. He says it
to frighten you, child.

Garth. Oh, no I don't! I say it
because I've held it in too long! I'm damned
if I sit here forever, and look at the door,
waiting for Trock with his sub-machine gun, waiting
for police with a warrant!—I say I'm damned, and I am,
no matter what I do! These piddling scales
on a violin—first position, third, fifth,
arpeggios in E—and what I'm thinking
is Romagna dead for the murder—dead while I sat here
dying inside—dead for the thing Trock did
while I looked on—and I could have saved him, yes—
but I sat here and let him die instead of me
because I wanted to live! Well, it's no life,
and it doesn't matter who I tell, because
I mean to get it over!

Miriamne. Garth, it's not true!

Garth. I'd take some scum down with me if I died—
that'd be one good deed—

Esdras. Son, son, you're mad—
someone will hear—

Garth. Then let them hear! I've lived
  with ghosts too long, and lied too long. God damn you
  if you keep me from the truth!—

  [*He turns away*]

  Oh, God damn the world!
I don't want to die!

  [*He throws himself down*]

Esdras. I should have known.
  I thought you hard and sullen,
  Garth, my son. And you were a child, and hurt
  with a wound that might be healed.
  —All men have crimes,
  and most of them are hidden, and many are heavy
  as yours must be to you.

  [Garth *sobs*]

  They walk the streets
  to buy and sell, but a spreading crimson stain
  tinges the inner vestments, touches flesh,
  and burns the quick. You're not alone.

Garth. I'm alone
  in this.

Esdras. Yes, if you hold with the world that only
  those who die suddenly should be revenged.
  But those whose hearts are cancered, drop by drop
  in small ways, little by little, till they've borne
  all they can bear, and die—these deaths will go
  unpunished now as always. When we're young
  we have faith in what is seen, but when we're old

we know that what is seen is traced in air
and built on water. There's no guilt under heaven,
just as there's no heaven, till men believe it—
no earth, till men have seen it, and have a word
to say this is the earth.

Garth. Well, I say there's an earth,
and I say I'm guilty on it, guilty as hell.

Esdras. Yet till it's known you bear no guilt at all—
unless you wish. The days go by like film,
like a long written scroll, a figured veil
unrolling out of darkness into fire
and utterly consumed. And on this veil,
running in sounds and symbols of men's minds
reflected back, life flickers and is shadow
going toward flame. Only what men can see
exists in that shadow. Why must you rise and cry out:
That was I, there in the ravelled tapestry,
there, in that pistol flash, when the man was killed.
I was there, and was one, and am bloodstained!
Let the wind
and fire take that hour to ashes out of time
and out of mind! This thing that men call justice,
this blind snake that strikes men down in the dark,
mindless with fury, keep your hand back from it,
pass by in silence—let it be forgotten, forgotten!—
Oh, my son, my son—have pity!

Miriamne. But if it was true
and someone died—then it was more than shadow—
and it doesn't blow away—

Garth. Well, it was true.

Esdras. Say it if you must. If you have heart to die,
    say it, and let them take what's left—there was little
    to keep, even before—

Garth. Oh, I'm a coward—
    I always was. I'll be quiet and live. I'll live
    even if I have to crawl. I know.

    [*He gets up and goes into the inner room*]

Miriamne. Is it better
    to tell a lie and live?

Esdras. Yes, child. It's better.

Miriamne. But if I had to do it—
    I think I'd die.

Esdras. Yes, child. Because you're young.

Miriamne. Is that the only reason?

Esdras. The only reason.

CURTAIN

ACT ONE

Scene III

Scene: *Under the bridge, evening of the same day. When the curtain rises* Miriamne *is sitting alone on the ledge at the rear of the apartment house. A spray of light falls on her from a street lamp above. She shivers a little in her thin coat, but sits still as if heedless of the weather. Through the rocks on the other side a* Tramp *comes down to the river bank, hunting a place to sleep. He goes softly to the apple-woman's hut and looks in, then turns away, evidently not daring to preëmpt it. He looks at Miriamne doubtfully. The door of the street-piano man is shut. The vagabond passes it and picks carefully among some rags and shavings to the right.* Miriamne *looks up and sees him but makes no sign. She looks down again, and the man curls himself up in a makeshift bed in the corner, pulling a piece of sacking over his shoulders.* Two Girls *come in from round the apartment house.*

1st Girl. Honest, I never heard of anything so romantic. Because you never liked him.

2nd Girl. I certainly never did.

1st Girl. You've got to tell me how it happened. You've got to.

2nd Girl. I couldn't. As long as I live I couldn't. Honest, it was terrible. It was terrible.

1st Girl. What was so terrible?

2nd Girl. The way it happened.

1st Girl. Oh, please—not to a soul, never.

21

2nd Girl. Well, you know how I hated him because he had such a big mouth. So he reached over and grabbed me, and I began all falling to pieces inside, the way you do—and I said, "Oh no you don't mister," and started screaming and kicked a hole through the windshield and lost a shoe, and he let go and was cursing and growling because he borrowed the car and didn't have money to pay for the windshield, and he started to cry, and I got so sorry for him I let him, and now he wants to marry me.

1st Girl. Honest, I never heard of anything so romantic!

> [*She sees the sleeping Tramp*]

My God, what you won't see!

> [*They give the Tramp a wide berth, and go out right. The* TRAMP *sits up looking about him.* JUDGE GAUNT, *an elderly, quiet man, well dressed but in clothes that have seen some weather, comes in uncertainly from the left. He holds a small clipping in his hand and goes up to the Hobo*]

Gaunt.

> [*Tentatively*]

Your pardon, sir. Your pardon, but perhaps you can tell me the name of this street.

Hobo. Huh?

Gaunt. The name of this street?

Hobo. This ain't no street.

Gaunt. There, where the street lamps are.

Hobo. That's the alley.

Gaunt. Thank you. It has a name, no doubt?

Hobo. That's the alley.

Gaunt. I see. I won't trouble you. You wonder why I ask, I daresay.—I'm a stranger.—Why do you look at me?

[*He steps back*]

I—I'm not the man you think. You've mistaken me, sir.

Hobo. Huh?

Judge. Perhaps misled by a resemblance. But you're mistaken—I had an errand in this city. It's only by accident that I'm here—

Hobo.

[*Muttering*]

You go to hell.

Judge.

[*Going nearer to him, bending over him*]

Yet why should I deceive you? Before God, I held the proofs in my hands. I hold them still. I tell you the defense was cunning beyond belief, and unscrupulous in its use of propaganda—they gagged at nothing—not even—

[*He rises*]

No, no—I'm sorry—this will hardly interest you. I'm sorry. I have an errand.

[*He looks toward the street.* ESDRAS *enters from the basement and goes to Miriamne. The* JUDGE *steps back into the shadows*]

Esdras. Come in, my daughter. You'll be cold here.

Miriamne. After a while.

Esdras. You'll be cold. There's a storm coming.

Miriamne. I didn't want him to see me crying. That was all.

Esdras. I know.

Miriamne. I'll come soon.

> [Esdras *turns reluctantly and goes out the way he came.* Miriamne *rises to go in, pausing to dry her eyes.* Mio *and* Carr, *road boys of seventeen or so, come round the apartment house. The Judge has disappeared*]

Carr. Thought you said you were never coming east again.

Mio. Yeah, but—I heard something changed my mind.

Carr. Same old business?

Mio. Yes. Just as soon not talk about it.

Carr. Where did you go from Portland?

Mio. Fishing—I went fishing. God's truth.

Carr. Right after I left?

Mio. Fell in with a fisherman's family on the coast and went after the beautiful mackerel fish that swim in the beautiful sea. Family of Greeks—Aristides Marinos was his lovely name. He sang while he fished. Made the pea-green Pacific ring with his bastard Greek chanties. Then I went to Hollywood High School for a while.

Carr. I'll bet that's a seat of learning.

Mio. It's the hind end of all wisdom. They kicked me out after a time.

Carr. For cause?

Mio. Because I had no permanent address, you see. That means nobody's paying school taxes for you, so out you go.
  [*To Miriamne*]
What's the matter, kid?

Mariamne. Nothing.
  [*She looks up at him, and they pause for a moment*]
Nothing.

Mio. I'm sorry.

Miriamne. It's all right.
  [*She withdraws her eyes from his and goes out past him. He turns and looks after her*]

Carr. Control your chivalry.

Mio. A pretty kid.

Carr. A baby.

Mio. Wait for me.

Carr. Be a long wait?
  [*Mio steps swiftly out after Miriamne, then returns*]
Yeah?

Mio. She's gone.

Carr. Think of that.

Mio. No, but I mean—vanished. Presto—into nothing—
prodigioso.

Carr. Damn good thing, if you ask me. The homely ones
are bad enough, but the lookers are fatal.

Mio. You exaggerate, Carr.

Carr. I doubt it.

Mio. Well, let her go. This river bank's loaded with typhus
rats, too. Might as well die one death as another.

Carr. They say chronic alcoholism is nice but expensive.
You can always starve to death.

Mio. Not always. I tried it. After the second day I walked
thirty miles to Niagara Falls and made a tour of the
plant to get the sample of shredded wheat biscuit on the
way out.

Carr. Last time I saw you you couldn't think of anything
you wanted to do except curse God and pass out. Still
feeling low?

Mio. Not much different.

[*He turns away, then comes back*]

Talk about the lost generation, I'm the only one fits
that title. When the State executes your father, and your
mother dies of grief, and you know damn well he was
innocent, and the authorities of your home town po-
litely inform you they'd consider it a favor if you lived
somewhere else—that cuts you off from the world—
with a meat-axe.

Carr. They asked you to move?

Mio. It came to that.

Carr. God, that was white of them.

Mio. It probably gave them a headache just to see me after all that agitation. They knew as well as I did my father never staged a holdup. Anyway, I've got a new interest in life now.

Carr. Yes—I saw her.

Mio. I don't mean the skirt.—No, I got wind of something, out west, some college professor investigating the trial and turning up new evidence. Couldn't find anything he'd written out there, so I beat it east and arrived on this blessed island just in time to find the bums holing up in the public library for the winter. I know now what the unemployed have been doing since the depression started. They've been catching up on their reading in the main reference room. Man, what a stench! Maybe I stank, too, but a hobo has the stench of ten because his shoes are poor.

Carr. Tennyson.

Mio. Right. Jeez, I'm glad we met up again! Never knew anybody else that could track me through the driven snow of Victorian literature.

Carr. Now you're cribbing from some half-forgotten criticism of Ben Jonson's Roman plagiarisms.

Mio. Where did you get your education, sap?

Carr. Not in the public library, sap. My father kept a news-stand.

Mio. Well, you're right again.

[*There is a faint rumble of thunder*]

What's that? Winter thunder?

Carr. Or Mister God, beating on His little tocsin. Maybe announcing the advent of a new social order.

Mio. Or maybe it's going to rain coffee and doughnuts.

Carr. Or maybe it's going to rain.

Mio. Seems more likely.

[*Lowering his voice*]

Anyhow, I found Professor Hobhouse's discussion of the Romagna case. I think he has something. It occurred to me I might follow it up by doing a little sleuthing on my own account.

Carr. Yes?

Mio. I have done a little. And it leads me to somewhere in that tenement house that backs up against the bridge. That's how I happen to be here.

Carr. They'll never let you get anywhere with it, Mio. I told you that before.

Mio. I know you did.

Carr. The State can't afford to admit it was wrong, you see. Not when there's been that much of a row kicked up over it. So for all practical purposes the State was right and your father robbed the pay roll.

Mio. There's still such a thing as evidence.

Carr. It's something you can buy. In fact, at the moment
   I don't think of anything you can't buy, including life,
   honor, virtue, glory, public office, conjugal affection and
   all kinds of justice, from the traffic court to the immortal
   nine. Go out and make yourself a pot of money and you
   can buy all the justice you want. Convictions obtained,
   convictions averted. Lowest rates in years.

Mio. I know all that.

Carr. Sure.

Mio. This thing didn't happen to you.
   They've left you your name
   and whatever place you can take. For my heritage
   they've left me one thing only, and that's to be
   my father's voice crying up out of the earth
   and quicklime where they stuck him. Electrocution
   doesn't kill, you know. They eviscerate them
   with a turn of the knife in the dissecting room.
   The blood spurts out. The man was alive. Then into
   the lime pit, leave no trace. Make it short shrift
   and chemical dissolution. That's what they thought
   of the man that was my father. Then my mother—
   I tell you these county burials are swift
   and cheap and run for profit! Out of the house
   and into the ground, you wife of a dead dog. Wait,
   here's some Romagna spawn left.
   Something crawls here—
   something they called a son. Why couldn't he die
   along with his mother? Well, ease him out of town,

ease him out, boys, and see you're not too gentle.
He might come back. And, by their own living Jesus,
I will go back, and hang the carrion
around their necks that made it!
Maybe I can sleep then.
Or even live.

Carr. You have to try it?

Mio. Yes.
Yes. It won't let me alone. I've tried to live
and forget it—but I was birthmarked with hot iron
into the entrails. I've got to find out who did it
and make them see it till it scalds their eyes
and make them admit it till their tongues are blistered
with saying how black they lied!

[HERMAN, *a gawky shoe salesman, enters from the left*]

Herman. Hello. Did you see a couple of girls go this way?

Carr. Couple of girls? Did we see a couple of girls?

Mio. No.

Carr. No. No girls.

[HERMAN *hesitates, then goes out right.* LUCIA *comes in from the left, trundling his piano.* PINY *follows him, weeping*]

Piny. They've got no right to do it—

Lucia. All right, hell what, no matter, I got to put him away, I got to put him away, that's what the hell!

[Two STREET URCHINS *follow him in*]

Piny. They want everybody on the relief rolls and nobody making a living?

Lucia. The cops, they do what the big boss says. The big boss, that's the mayor, he says he heard it once too often, the sextette—

Piny. They want graft, that's all. It's a new way to get graft—

Lucia. Oh, no, no, no! He's a good man, the mayor. He's just don't care for music, that's all.

Piny. Why shouldn't you make a living on the street? The National Biscuit Company ropes off Eighth Avenue—and does the mayor do anything? No, the police hit you over the head if you try to go through!

Lucia. You got the big dough, you get the pull, fine. No big dough, no pull, what the hell, get off the city property! Tomorrow I start cooking chestnuts . . .

[*He strokes the piano fondly. The* Two Girls *and* Herman *come back from the right*]

She's a good little machine, this baby. Cost plenty—and two new records I only played twice. See, this one.

[*He starts turning the crank, talking while he plays*]

Two weeks since they play this one in a picture house.

[A Sailor *wanders in from the left. One of the* Street Urchins *begins suddenly to dance a wild rumba, the others watch*]

Good boy—see, it's a lulu—it itches in the feet!

[Herman, *standing with his girl, tosses the boy a penny. He bows and goes on dancing; the other* Urchin *joins him. The* Sailor *tosses a coin*]

Sailor. Go it, Cuba! Go it!

[Lucia *turns the crank, beaming*]

2nd Girl. Oh, Herman!

[*She throws her arms round Herman and they dance*]

1st Urchin. Hey, pipe the professionals!

1st Girl. Do your glide, Shirley! Do your glide!

Lucia. Maybe we can't play in front, maybe we can play
behind!

[*The* Hobo *gets up from his nest and comes over to watch.
A* Young Radical *wanders in*]

Maybe you don't know, folks! Tonight we play good-
bye to the piano! Good-bye forever! No more piano on
the streets! No more music! No more money for the
music-man! Last time, folks! Good-bye to the piano—
good-bye forever!

[Miriamne *comes out the rear door of the apartment and stands
watching. The* Sailor *goes over to the 1st Girl and they
dance together*]

Maybe you don't know, folks! Tomorrow will be sad as
hell, tonight we dance! Tomorrow no more Verdi, no
more rumba, no more good time! Tonight we play good-
bye to the piano, good-bye forever!

[*The* Radical *edges up to Miriamne, and asks her to dance.
She shakes her head and he goes to Piny, who dances
with him. The* Hobo *begins to do a few lonely curvets
on the side above*]

Hoy! Hoy! Pick 'em up and take 'em around! Use the
head, use the feet! Last time forever!

[*He begins to sing to the air*]

Mio. Wait for me, will you?

Carr. Now's your chance.

> [MIO *goes over to Miriamne and holds out a hand, smiling.*
> *She stands for a moment uncertain, then dances with*
> *him.* ESDRAS *comes out to watch.* JUDGE GAUNT *comes*
> *in from the left. There is a rumble of thunder*]

Lucia. Hoy! Hoy! Maybe it rains tonight, maybe it snows tomorrow! Tonight we dance good-bye.

> [*He sings the air lustily.* A POLICEMAN *comes in from the left*
> *and looks on.* TWO OR THREE PEDESTRIANS *follow*
> *him*]

Policeman. Hey you!

> [LUCIA *goes on singing*]

Hey, you!

Lucia.

> [*Still playing*]

What you want?

Policeman. Sign off!

Lucia. What you mean? I get off the street!

Policeman. Sign off!

Lucia.

> [*Still playing*]

What you mean?

> [*The* POLICEMAN *walks over to him.* LUCIA *stops playing and*
> *the* DANCERS *pause*]

Policeman. Cut it.

Lucia. Is this a street?

Policeman. I say cut it out.

[*The* HOBO *goes back to his nest and sits in it, watching*]

Lucia. It's the last time. We dance good-bye to the piano.

Policeman. You'll dance good-bye to something else if I catch you cranking that thing again.

Lucia. All right.

Piny. I'll bet you don't say that to the National Biscuit Company!

Policeman. Lady, you've been selling apples on my beat for some time now, and I said nothing about it—

Piny. Selling apples is allowed—

Policeman. You watch yourself—

[*He takes a short walk around the place and comes upon the Hobo*]

What are you doing here?

[*The* HOBO *opens his mouth, points to it, and shakes his head*]

Oh, you are, are you?

[*He comes back to Lucia*]

So you trundle your so-called musical instrument to wherever you keep it, and don't let me hear it again.

[*The* RADICAL *leaps on the base of the rock at right. The* 1ST GIRL *turns away from the Sailor toward the 2nd Girl and Herman*]

Sailor. Hey, captain, what's the matter with the music?

Policeman. Not a thing, admiral.

Sailor. Well, we had a little party going here—

Policeman. I'll say you did.

2nd Girl. Please, officer, we want to dance.

Policeman. Go ahead. Dance.

2nd Girl. But we want music!

Policeman.
   [*Turning to go*]
   Sorry. Can't help you.

Radical. And there you see it, the perfect example of capitalistic oppression! In a land where music should be free as air and the arts should be encouraged, a uniformed minion of the rich, a guardian myrmidon of the Park Avenue pleasure hunters, steps in and puts a limit on the innocent enjoyments of the poor! We don't go to theatres! Why not? We can't afford it! We don't go to night clubs, where women dance naked and the music drips from saxophones and leaks out of Rudy Vallee— we can't afford that either!—But we might at least dance on the river bank to the strains of a barrel organ—!

   [GARTH *comes out of the apartment and listens*]

Policeman. It's against the law!

Radical. What law? I challenge you to tell me what law of God or man—what ordinance—is violated by this spontaneous diversion? None! I say none! An official whim of the masters who should be our servants!—

Policeman. Get down! Get down and shut up!

Radical. By what law, by what ordinance do you order me to be quiet?

Policeman. Speaking without a flag. You know it.

Radical.

[*Pulling out a small American flag*]

There's my flag! There's the flag of this United States which used to guarantee the rights of man—the rights of man now violated by every third statute of the commonweal—

Policeman. Don't try to pull tricks on me! I've seen you before! You're not making any speech, and you're climbing down—

Judge Gaunt.

[*Who has come quietly forward*]

One moment, officer. There is some difference of opinion even on the bench as to the elasticity of police power when applied in minor emergencies to preserve civil order. But the weight of authority would certainly favor the defendant in any equable court, and he would be upheld in his demand to be heard.

Policeman. Who are you?

Judge Gaunt. Sir, I am not accustomed to answer that question.

Policeman. I don't know you.

Gaunt. I am a judge of some standing, not in your city but in another with similar statutes. You are aware, of

course, that the bill of rights is not to be set aside lightly
by the officers of any municipality—

Policeman.

[*Looking over Gaunt's somewhat bedraggled costume*]

Maybe they understand you better in the town you come
from, but I don't get your drift.—

[*To the Radical*]

I don't want any trouble, but if you ask for it you'll
get plenty. Get down!

Radical. I'm not asking for trouble, but I'm staying right
here.

[*The* POLICEMAN *moves toward him*]

Gaunt.

[*Taking the policeman's arm, but shaken off roughly*]

I ask this for yourself, truly, not for the dignity of the
law nor the maintenance of precedent. Be gentle with
them when their threats are childish—be tolerant while
you can—for your least harsh word will return on you
in the night—return in a storm of cries!—

[*He takes the Policeman's arm again*]

Whatever they may have said or done, let them disperse
in peace! It is better that they go softly, lest when they
are dead you see their eyes pleading, and their out-
stretched hands touch you, fingering cold on your heart!
—I have been harsher than you. I have sent men down
that long corridor into blinding light and blind darkness!

[*He suddenly draws himself erect and speaks defiantly*]

And it was well that I did so! I have been an upright judge! They are all liars! Liars!

Policeman.

[*Shaking* GAUNT *off so that he falls*]

Why, you fool, you're crazy!

Gaunt. Yes, and there are liars on the force! They came to me with their shifty lies!

[*He catches at the* POLICEMAN, *who pushes him away with his foot*]

Policeman. You think I've got nothing better to do than listen to a crazy fool?

1st Girl. Shame, shame!

Policeman. What have I got to be ashamed of? And what's going on here, anyway? Where in hell did you all come from?

Radical. Tread on him! That's right! Tread down the poor and the innocent!

[*There is a protesting murmur in the crowd*]

Sailor.

[*Moving in a little*]

Say, big boy, you don't have to step on the guy.

Policeman.

[*Facing them, stepping back*]

What's the matter with you? I haven't stepped on anybody!

Mio.

    [*At the right, across from the Policeman*]

Listen now, fellows, give the badge a chance.
He's doing his job, what he gets paid to do,
the same as any of you. They're all picked men,
these metropolitan police, hand picked
for loyalty and a fine up-standing pair
of shoulders on their legs—it's not so easy
to represent the law. Think what he does
for all of us, stamping out crime!
Do you want to be robbed and murdered in your beds?

Sailor. What's eating you?

Radical. He must be a capitalist.

Mio. They pluck them fresh
from Ireland, and a paucity of headpiece
is a prime prerequisite. You from Ireland, buddy?

Policeman.

    [*Surly*]

Where are you from?

Mio. Buddy, I tell you flat
I wish I was from Ireland, and could boast
some Tammany connections. There's only one drawback
about working on the force. It infects the brain,
it eats the cerebrum. There've been cases known,
fine specimens of manhood, too, where autopsies,
conducted in approved scientific fashion,
revealed conditions quite incredible

in policemen's upper layers. In some, a trace,
in others, when they've swung a stick too long,
there was nothing there!—but nothing! Oh, my friends,
this fine athletic figure of a man
that stands so grim before us, what will they find
when they saw his skull for the last inspection?
I fear me a little puffball dust will blow away
rejoining earth, our mother—and this same dust,
this smoke, this ash on the wind, will represent
all he had left to think with!

The Hobo. Hooray!

    [*The* POLICEMAN *turns on his heel and looks hard at the* HOBO,
      who slinks away]

Policeman. Oh, yeah?

Mio. My theme
gives ears to the deaf and voice to the dumb! But now
forgive me if I say you were most unkind
in troubling the officer. He's a simple man
of simple tastes, and easily confused
when faced with complex issues. He may reflect
on returning home, that is, so far as he
is capable of reflection, and conclude
that he was kidded out of his uniform pants,
and in his fury when this dawns on him
may smack his wife down!

Policeman. That'll be about enough from you, too, professor!

Mio. May I say that I think you have managed this whole
situation rather badly, from the beginning?—

Policeman. You may not!

> [T<small>ROCK</small> *slips in from the background. The* T<small>WO</small> Y<small>OUNG</small> M<small>EN</small> <small>IN</small> S<small>ERGE</small> *come with him*]

Mio. Oh, but your pardon, sir! It's apparent to the least competent among us that you should have gone about your task more subtly—the glove of velvet, the hand of iron, and all that sort of thing—

Policeman. Shut that hole in your face!

Mio. Sir, for that remark I shall be satisfied with nothing less than an unconditional apology! I have an old score to settle with policemen, brother, because they're fools and fat-heads, and you're one of the most fatuous fat-heads that ever walked his feet flat collecting graft! Tell that to your sergeant back in the booby-hatch.

Policeman. Oh, you want an apology, do you? You'll get an apology out of the other side of your mouth!

> [*He steps toward Mio.* C<small>ARR</small> *suddenly stands in his path*]

Get out of my way!

> [*He pauses and looks round him; the crowd looks less and less friendly. He lays a hand on his gun and backs to a position where there is nobody behind him*]

Get out of here, all of you! Get out! What are you trying to do—start a riot?

Mio. There now, that's better! That's in the best police tradition. Incite a riot yourself and then accuse the crowd.

Policeman. It won't be pleasant if I decide to let somebody have it! Get out!

[*The onlookers begin to melt away. The* SAILOR *goes out left
with the* GIRLS *and* HERMAN. CARR *and* MIO *go out
right,* CARR *whistling "The Star Spangled Banner." The*
HOBO *follows them. The* RADICAL *walks past with his
head in the air.* PINY *and* LUCIA *leave the piano where
it stands and slip away to the left. At the end the* POLICE-
MAN *is left standing in the center, the* JUDGE *near him.*
ESDRAS *stands in the doorway.* MIRIAMNE *is left
sitting half in shadow and unseen by* ESDRAS]

Judge Gaunt.

[*To the Policeman*]

Yes, but should a man die, should it be necessary that
one man die for the good of many, make not yourself
the instrument of death, lest you sleep to wake sobbing!
Nay, it avails nothing that you are the law—this delicate ganglion that is the brain, it will not bear these
things—!

[*The* POLICEMAN *gives the Judge the once-over, shrugs, decides
to leave him there and starts out left.* GARTH *goes to his
father—a fine sleet begins to fall through the street lights.*
TROCK *is still visible*]

Garth. Get him in here, quick.

Esdras. Who, son?

Garth. The Judge, damn him!

Esdras. Is it Judge Gaunt?

Garth. Who did you think it was? He's crazy as a bedbug
and telling the world. Get him inside!

[*He looks round*]

Esdras.

[*Going up to Gaunt*]

Will you come in, sir?

Gaunt. You will understand, sir. We old men know how softly we must proceed with these things.

Esdras. Yes, surely, sir.

Gaunt. It was always my practice—always. They will tell you that of me where I am known. Yet even I am not free of regret—even I. Would you believe it?

Esdras. I believe we are none of us free of regret.

Gaunt. None of us? I would it were true. I would I thought it were true.

Esdras. Shall we go in, sir? This is sleet that's falling.

Gaunt. Yes. Let us go in.

> [Esdras, Gaunt *and* Garth *enter the basement and shut the door.* Trock *goes out with his men. After a pause* Mio *comes back from the right, alone. He stands at a little distance from Miriamne*]

Mio. Looks like rain.

> [*She is silent*]

You live around here?

> [*She nods gravely*]

I guess
you thought I meant it—about waiting here to meet me.

> [*She nods again*]

I'd forgotten about it till I got that winter
across the face. You'd better go inside.

I'm not your kind. I'm nobody's kind but my own.
I'm waiting for this to blow over.

   [*She rises*]

   I lied. I meant it—
I meant it when I said it—but there's too much black
whirling inside me—for any girl to know.
So go on in. You're somebody's angel child
and they're waiting for you.

Miriamne. Yes. I'll go.

   [*She turns*]

Mio. And tell them
when you get inside where it's warm,
and you love each other,
and mother comes to kiss her darling, tell them
to hang on to it while they can, believe while they can
it's a warm safe world, and Jesus finds his lambs
and carries them in his bosom.—I've seen some lambs
that Jesus missed. If they ever want the truth
tell them that nothing's guaranteed in this climate
except it gets cold in winter, nor on this earth
except you die sometime.

   [*He turns away*]

Miriamne. I have no mother.
And my people are Jews.

Mio. Then you know something about it.

Miriamne. Yes.

Mio. Do you have enough to eat?

Miriamne. Not always.

Mio. What do you believe in?

Miriamne. Nothing.

Mio. Why?

Miriamne. How can one?

Mio. It's easy if you're a fool. You see the words
in books. Honor, it says there, chivalry, freedom,
heroism, enduring love—and these
are words on paper. It's something to have them there.
You'll get them nowhere else.

Miriamne. What hurts you?

Mio. Just that.
You'll get them nowhere else.

Miriamne. Why should you want them?

Mio. I'm alone, that's why. You see those lights,
along the river, cutting across the rain—?
those are the hearths of Brooklyn, and up this way
the love-nests of Manhattan—they turn their points
like knives against me—outcast of the world,
snake in the streets.—I don't want a hand-out.
I sleep and eat.

Miriamne. Do you want me to go with you?

Mio. Where?

Miriamne. Where you go.

[*A pause. He goes nearer to her*]

Mio. Why, you god-damned little fool—
    what made you say that?

Miriamne. I don't know.

Mio. If you have a home
    stay in it. I ask for nothing. I've schooled myself
    to ask for nothing, and take what I can get,
    and get along. If I fell for you, that's my look-out,
    and I'll starve it down.

Miriamne. Wherever you go, I'd go.

Mio. What do you know about loving?
    How could you know?
    Have you ever had a man?

Miriamne.

    [*After a slight pause*]

    No. But I know.
    Tell me your name.

Mio. Mio. What's yours?

Miriamne. Miriamne.

Mio. There's no such name.

Miriamne. But there's no such name as Mio!
    M.I.O. It's no name.

Mio. It's for Bartolomeo.

Miriamne. My mother's name was Miriam,
    so they called me Miriamne.

Mio. Meaning little Miriam?

Miriamne. Yes.

Mio. So now little Miriamne will go in
    and take up quietly where she dropped them all
    her small housewifely cares.—When I first saw you,
    not a half-hour ago, I heard myself saying,
    this is the face that launches ships for me—
    and if I owned a dream—yes, half a dream—
    we'd share it. But I have no dream. This earth
    came tumbling down from chaos, fire and rock,
    and bred up worms, blind worms that sting each other
    here in the dark. These blind worms of the earth
    took out my father—and killed him, and set a sign
    on me—the heir of the serpent—and he was a man
    such as men might be if the gods were men—
    but they killed him—
    as they'll kill all others like him
    till the sun cools down to the stabler molecules,
    yes, till men spin their tent-worm webs to the stars
    and what they think is done, even in the thinking,
    and they are the gods, and immortal, and constellations
    turn for them all like mill wheels—still as they are
    they will be, worms and blind. Enduring love,
    oh gods and worms, what mockery!—And yet
    I have blood enough in my veins. It goes like music,
    singing, because you're here. My body turns
    as if you were the sun, and warm. This men called love
    in happier times, before the Freudians taught us
    to blame it on the glands. Only go in
    before you breathe too much of my atmosphere
    and catch death from me.

Miriamne. I will take my hands
and weave them to a little house, and there
you shall keep a dream—

Mio. God knows I could use a dream
and even a house.

Miriamne. You're laughing at me, Mio!

Mio. The worms are laughing.
I tell you there's death about me
and you're a child! And I'm alone and half mad
with hate and longing. I shall let you love me
and love you in return, and then, why then
God knows what happens!

Miriamne. Something most unpleasant?

Mio. Love in a box car—love among the children.
I've seen too much of it. Are we to live
in this same house you make with your two hands
mystically, out of air?

Miriamne. No roof, no mortgage!
Well, I shall marry a baker out in Flatbush,
it gives hot bread in the morning! Oh, Mio, Mio,
in all the unwanted places and waste lands
that roll up into the darkness out of sun
and into sun out of dark, there should be one empty
for you and me.

Mio. No.

Miriamne. Then go now and leave me.
I'm only a girl you saw in the tenements,
and there's been nothing said.

Mio. Miriamne.

[*She takes a step toward him*]

Miriamne. Yes.

[*He kisses her lips lightly*]

Mio. Why, girl, the transfiguration on the mount
was nothing to your face. It lights from within—
a white chalice holding fire, a flower in flame,
this is your face.

Miriamne. And you shall drink the flame
and never lessen it. And round your head
the aureole shall burn that burns there now,
forever. This I can give you. And so forever
the Freudians are wrong.

Mio. They're well-forgotten
at any rate.

Miriamne. Why did you speak to me
when you first saw me?

Mio. I knew then.

Miriamne. And I came back
because I must see you again. And we danced together
and my heart hurt me. Never, never, never,
though they should bind me down and tear out my eyes,
would I ever hurt you now. Take me with you, Mio,
let them look for us, whoever there is to look,
but we'll be away.

[Mio *turns away toward the tenement*]

Mio. When I was four years old
we climbed through an iron gate, my mother and I,
to see my father in prison. He stood in the death-cell
and put his hand through the bars and said, My Mio,
I have only this to leave you, that I love you,
and will love you after I die. Love me then, Mio,
when this hard thing comes on you, that you must live
a man despised for your father. That night the guards,
walking in flood-lights brighter than high noon,
led him between them with his trousers slit
and a shaven head for the cathodes. This sleet and rain
that I feel cold here on my face and hands
will find him under thirteen years of clay
in prison ground. Lie still and rest, my father,
for I have not forgotten. When I forget
may I lie blind as you. No other love,
time passing, nor the spaced light-years of suns
shall blur your voice, or tempt me from the path
that clears your name—
till I have these rats in my grip
or sleep deep where you sleep.

   [*To Miriamne*]

   I have no house,
nor home, nor love of life, nor fear of death,
nor care for what I eat, or who I sleep with,
or what color of calcimine the Government
will wash itself this year or next to lure
the sheep and feed the wolves. Love somewhere else,
and get your children in some other image
more acceptable to the State! This face of mine
is stamped for sewage!

[*She steps back, surmising*]

Miriamne. Mio—

Mio. My road is cut
in rock, and leads to one end. If I hurt you, I'm sorry.
One gets over hurts.

Miriamne. What was his name—
your father's name?

Mio. Bartolomeo Romagna.
I'm not ashamed of it.

Miriamne. Why are you here?

Mio. For the reason
I've never had a home. Because I'm a cry
out of a shallow grave, and all roads are mine
that might revenge him!

Miriamne. But Mio—why here—why here?

Mio. I can't tell you that.

Miriamne. No—but—there's someone
lives here—lives not far—and you mean to see him—
you mean to ask him—

[*She pauses*]

Mio. Who told you that?

Miriamne. His name
is Garth—Garth Esdras—

Mio.

[*After a pause, coming nearer*]

Who are you, then? You seem
to know a good deal about me.—Were you sent
to say this?

Miriamne. You said there was death about you! Yes,
but nearer than you think! Let it be as it is—
let it all be as it is, never see this place
nor think of it—forget the streets you came
when you're away and safe! Go before you're seen
or spoken to!

Mio. Will you tell me why?

Miriamne. As I love you
I can't tell you—and I can never see you—

Mio. I walk where I please—

Miriamne. Do you think it's easy for me
to send you away?

[*She steps back as if to go*]

Mio. Where will I find you then
if I should want to see you?

Miriamne. Never—I tell you
I'd bring you death! Even now. Listen!

[Shadow *and* Trock *enter between the bridge and the tenement
house.* Miriamne *pulls* Mio *back into the shadow of the
rock to avoid being seen*]

Trock. Why, fine.

Shadow. You watch it now—just for the record, Trock—
you're going to thank me for staying away from it
and keeping you out. I've seen men get that way,

thinking they had to plug a couple of guys
and then a few more to cover it up, and then
maybe a dozen more. You can't own all
and territory adjacent, and you can't
slough all the witnesses, because every man
you put away has friends—

Trock. I said all right.
I said fine.

Shadow. They're going to find this judge,
and if they find him dead it's just too bad,
and I don't want to know anything about it—
and you don't either.

Trock. You all through?

Shadow. Why sure.

Trock. All right.
We're through, too, you know.

Shadow. Yeah?

[*He becomes wary*]

Trock. Yeah, we're through.

Shadow. I've heard that said before, and afterwards
somebody died.

[TROCK *is silent*]

Is that what you mean?

Trock. You can go.
I don't want to see you.

Shadow. Sure, I'll go.
Maybe you won't mind if I just find out
what you've got on you. Before I turn my back
I'd like to know.

[*Silently and expertly he touches Trock's pockets, extracting a gun*]

Not that I'd distrust you,
but you know how it is.

[*He pockets the gun*]

So long, Trock.

Trock. So long.

Shadow. I won't talk.
You can be sure of that.

Trock. I know you won't.

[SHADOW *turns and goes out right, past the rock and along the bank. As he goes the* TWO YOUNG MEN IN BLUE SERGE *enter from the left and walk slowly after Shadow. They look toward Trock as they enter and he motions with his thumb in the direction taken by Shadow. They follow Shadow out without haste.* TROCK *watches them disappear, then slips out the way he came.* MIO *comes a step forward, looking after the two men. Two or three shots are heard, then silence.* MIO *starts to run after Shadow*]

Miriamne. Mio!

Mio. What do you know about this?

Miriamne. The other way,
Mio—quick!

[CARR *slips in from the right, in haste*]

Carr. Look, somebody's just been shot.
  He fell in the river. The guys that did the shooting
  ran up the bank.

Mio. Come on.

  [M<small>IO</small> *and* C<small>ARR</small> *run out right.* M<small>IRIAMNE</small> *watches uncertainly,
  then slowly turns and walks to the rear door of the
  tenement. She stands there a moment, looking after
  Mio, then goes in, closing the door.* C<small>ARR</small> *and* M<small>IO</small>
  return]

Carr. There's a rip tide past the point. You'd never find
  him.

Mio. No.

Carr. You know a man really ought to carry insurance
  living around here.—God, it's easy, putting a fellow
  away. I never saw it done before.

Mio.

  [*Looking at the place where Miriamne stood*]
  They have it all worked out.

Carr. What are you doing now?

Mio. I have a little business to transact in this neighbor-
  hood.

Carr. You'd better forget it.

Mio. No.

Carr. Need any help?

Mio. Well, if I did I'd ask you first. But I don't see how it
  would do any good. So you keep out of it and take care
  of yourself.

Carr. So long, then.

Mio. So long, Carr.

Carr.

> [*Looking down-stream*]

He was drifting face up. Must be halfway to the island the way the tide runs.

> [*He shivers*]

God, it's cold here. Well—

> [*He goes out to the left.* Mio *sits on the edge of the rock.* Lucia *comes stealthily back from between the bridge and the tenement, goes to the street-piano and wheels it away.* Piny *comes in. They take a look at Mio, but say nothing.* Lucia *goes into his shelter and* Piny *into hers.* Mio *rises, looks up at the tenement, and goes out to the left*]

CURTAIN

WINTERSET
ACT TWO

ACT TWO

SCENE: *The basement as in Scene 2 of Act One. The same evening.*
ESDRAS *sits at the table reading,* MIRIAMNE *is seated at the left,*
listening and intent. The door of the inner room is half open
and Garth's violin is heard. He is playing the theme from the
third movement of Beethoven's Archduke Trio. ESDRAS *looks*
up.

Esdras. I remember when I came to the end
of all the Talmud said, and the commentaries,
then I was fifty years old—and it was time
to ask what I had learned. I asked this question
and gave myself the answer. In all the Talmud
there was nothing to find but the names of things,
set down that we might call them by those names
and walk without fear among things known. Since then
I have had twenty years to read on and on
and end with Ecclesiastes. Names of names,
evanid days, evanid nights and days
and words that shift their meaning. Space is time,
that which was is now—the men of tomorrow
live, and this is their yesterday. All things
that were and are and will be, have their being
then and now and to come. If this means little
when you are young, remember it. It will return
to mean more when you are old.

Miriamne. I'm sorry—I
was listening for something.

Esdras. It doesn't matter.
It's a useless wisdom. It's all I have,

59

but useless. It may be there is no time,
but we grow old. Do you know his name?

Miriamne. Whose name?

Esdras. Why, when we're young and listen for a step
the step should have a name—

[MIRIAMNE, *not hearing, rises and goes to the window.* GARTH
*enters from within, carrying his violin and carefully
closing the door*]

Garth.

[*As* ESDRAS *looks at him*]

Asleep.

Esdras. He may
sleep on through the whole night—then in the morning
we can let them know.

Garth. We'd be wiser to say nothing—
let him find his own way back.

Esdras. How did he come here?

Garth. He's not too crazy for that. If he wakes again
we'll keep him quiet and shift him off tomorrow.
Somebody'd pick him up.

Esdras. How have I come
to this sunken end of a street, at a life's end—?

Garth. It was cheaper here—not to be transcendental—
So—we say nothing—?

Esdras. Nothing.

Miriamne. Garth, there's no place
 in this whole city—not one—
 where you wouldn't be safer
 than here—tonight—or tomorrow.

Garth.

 [*Bitterly*]

 Well, that may be.
 What of it?

Miriamne. If you slipped away and took
 a place somewhere where Trock couldn't find you—

Garth. Yes—
 using what for money? and why do you think
 I've sat here so far—because I love my home
 so much? No, but if I stepped round the corner
 it'd be my last corner and my last step.

Miriamne. And yet—
 if you're here—they'll find you here—
 Trock will come again—
 and there's worse to follow—

Garth. Do you want to get me killed?

Miriamne. No.

Garth. There's no way out of it. We'll wait
 and take what they send us.

Esdras. Hush! You'll wake him.

Garth. I've done it.
 I hear him stirring now.

 [*They wait quietly.* JUDGE GAUNT *opens the door and enters*]

Gaunt.

> [*In the doorway*]

I beg your pardon—
no, no, be seated—keep your place—I've made
your evening difficult enough, I fear;
and I must thank you doubly for your kindness,
for I've been ill—I know it.

Esdras. You're better, sir?

Gaunt. Quite recovered, thank you. Able, I hope,
to manage nicely now. You'll be rewarded
for your hospitality—though at this moment

> [*He smiles*]

I'm low in funds.

> [*He inspects his billfold*]

Sir, my embarrassment
is great indeed—and more than monetary,
for I must own my recollection's vague
of how I came here—how we came together—
and what we may have said. My name is Gaunt,
Judge Gaunt, a name long known in the criminal courts,
and not unhonored there.

Esdras. My name is Esdras—
and this is Garth, my son. And Miriamne,
the daughter of my old age.

Gaunt. I'm glad to meet you.
Esdras. Garth Esdras.

> [*He passes a hand over his eyes*]

It's not a usual name.
Of late it's been connected with a case—
a case I knew. But this is hardly the man.
Though it's not a usual name.

[*They are silent*]

Sir, how I came here,
as I have said, I don't well know. Such things
are sometimes not quite accident.

Esdras. We found you
outside our door and brought you in.

Gaunt. The brain
can be overworked, and weary, even when the man
would swear to his good health. Sir, on my word
I don't know why I came here, nor how, nor when,
nor what would explain it. Shall we say the machine
begins to wear? I felt no twinge of it.—
You will imagine how much more than galling
I feel it, to ask my way home—and where I am—
but I do ask you that.

Esdras. This is New York City—
or part of it.

Gaunt. Not the best part, I presume?

[*He smiles grimly*]

No, not the best.

Esdras. Not typical, no.

Gaunt. And you—

[*To Garth*]

you are Garth Esdras?

Garth. That's my name.

Gaunt. Well, sir,

   [*To Esdras*]

I shall lie under the deepest obligation
if you will set an old man on his path,
for I lack the homing instinct, if the truth
were known. North, east and south mean nothing to me
here in this room.

Esdras. I can put you in your way.

Garth. Only you'd be wiser to wait a while—
if I'm any judge.—

Gaunt. It happens I'm the judge—

   [*With stiff humor*]

in more ways than one. You'll forgive me if I say
I find this place and my predicament
somewhat distasteful.

   [*He looks round him*]

Garth. I don't doubt you do;
but you're better off here.

Gaunt. Nor will you find it wise
to cross my word as lightly as you seem
inclined to do. You've seen me ill and shaken—
and you presume on that.

Garth. Have it your way.

Gaunt. Doubtless what information is required
  we'll find nearby.

Esdras. Yes, sir—the terminal,—
  if you could walk so far.

Gaunt. I've done some walking—
  to look at my shoes.

  [*He looks down, then puts out a hand to steady himself*]

    That—that was why I came—
  never mind—it was there—and it's gone.

  [*To Garth*]

    Professor Hobhouse—
  that's the name—he wrote some trash about you
  and printed it in a broadside.
  —Since I'm here I can tell you
  it's a pure fabrication—lacking facts
  and legal import. Senseless and impudent,
  written with bias—with malicious intent
  to undermine the public confidence
  in justice and the courts. I knew it then—
  all he brings out about this testimony
  you might have given. It's true I could have called you,
  but the case was clear—Romagna was known guilty,
  and there was nothing to add. If I've endured
  some hours of torture over their attacks
  upon my probity—and in this torture
  have wandered from my place, wandered perhaps
  in mind and body—and found my way to face you—
  why, yes, it is so—I know it—I beg of you
  say nothing. It's not easy to give up

a fair name after a full half century
of service to a state. It may well rock
the surest reason. Therefore I ask of you
say nothing of this visit.

Garth. I'll say nothing.

Esdras. Nor any of us.

Gaunt. Why, no—for you'd lose, too.
You'd have nothing to gain.

Esdras. Indeed we know it.

Gaunt. I'll remember you kindly. When I've returned,
there may be some mystery made of where I was—
we'll leave it a mystery?

Garth. Anything you say.

Gaunt. Why, now I go with much more peace of mind—
if I can call you friends.

Esdras. We shall be grateful
for silence on your part, Your Honor.

Gaunt. Sir—
if there were any just end to be served
by speaking out, I'd speak! There is none. No—
bear that in mind!

Esdras. We will, Your Honor.

Gaunt. Then—
I'm in some haste. If you can be my guide,
we'll set out now.

Esdras. Yes, surely.

> [*There is a knock at the door. The four look at each other with some apprehension.* MIRIAMNE *rises*]

I'll answer it.

Miriamne. Yes.

> [*She goes into the inner room and closes the door.* ESDRAS *goes to the outer door. The knock is repeated. He opens the door.* MIO *is there*]

Esdras. Yes, sir.

Mio. May I come in?

Esdras. Will you state your business, sir?
It's late—and I'm not at liberty—

Mio. Why, I might say
that I was trying to earn my tuition fees
by peddling magazines. I could say that,
or collecting old newspapers—paying cash—
highest rates—no questions asked—

> [*He looks round sharply*]

Garth. We've nothing to sell.
What do you want?

Mio. Your pardon, gentlemen.
My business is not of an ordinary kind,
and I felt the need of this slight introduction
while I might get my bearings. Your name is Esdras,
or they told me so outside.

Garth. What do you want?

Mio. Is that the name?

Garth. Yes.

Mio. I'll be quick and brief.
I'm the son of a man who died many years ago
for a pay roll robbery in New England. You
should be Garth Esdras, by what I've heard. You have
some knowledge of the crime, if one can believe
what he reads in the public prints, and it might be
that your testimony, if given, would clear my father
of any share in the murder. You may not care
whether he was guilty or not. You may not know.
But I do care—and care deeply, and I've come
to ask you face to face.

Garth. To ask me what?

Mio. What do you know of it?

Esdras. This man Romagna,
did he have a son?

Mio. Yes, sir, this man Romagna,
as you choose to call him, had a son, and I
am that son, and proud.

Esdras. Forgive me.

Mio. Had you known him,
and heard him speak, you'd know why I'm proud,
and why
he was no malefactor.

Esdras. I quite believe you.
If my son can help he will. But at this moment,
as I told you—could you, I wonder, come tomorrow,
at your own hour?

Mio. Yes.

Esdras. By coincidence
    we too of late have had this thing in mind—
    there have been comments printed, and much discussion
    which we could hardly avoid.

Mio. Could you tell me then
    in a word?—What you know—
    is it for him or against him?—
    that's all I need.

Esdras. My son knows nothing.

Garth. No.
    The picture-papers lash themselves to a fury
    over any rumor—make them up when they're short
    of bedroom slops.—This is what happened. I
    had known a few members of a gang one time
    up there—and after the murder they picked me up
    because I looked like someone that was seen
    in what they called the murder car. They held me
    a little while, but they couldn't identify me
    for the most excellent reason I wasn't there
    when the thing occurred. A dozen years later now
    a professor comes across this, and sees red
    and asks why I wasn't called on as a witness
    and yips so loud they syndicate his picture
    in all the rotos. That's all I know about it.
    I wish I could tell you more.

Esdras. Let me say too
    that I have read some words your father said,

and you were a son fortunate in your father,
whatever the verdict of the world.

Mio. There are few
who think so, but it's true, and I thank you. Then—
that's the whole story?

Garth. All I know of it.

Mio. They cover their tracks well, the inner ring
that distributes murder. I came three thousand miles
to this dead end.

Esdras. If he was innocent
and you know him so, believe it, and let the others
believe as they like.

Mio. Will you tell me how a man's
to live, and face his life, if he can't believe
that truth's like a fire,
and will burn through and be seen
though it takes all the years there are?
While I stand up and have breath in my lungs
I shall be one flame of that fire;
it's all the life I have.

Esdras. Then you must live so.
One must live as he can.

Mio. It's the only way
of life my father left me.

Esdras. Yes? Yet it's true
the ground we walk on is impacted down
and hard with blood and bones of those who died

unjustly. There's not one title to land or life,
even your own, but was built on rape and murder,
back a few years. It would take a fire indeed
to burn out all this error.

Mio. Then let it burn down,
all of it!

Esdras. We ask a great deal of the world
at first—then less—and then less.
We ask for truth
and justice. But this truth's a thing unknown
in the lightest, smallest matter—and as for justice,
who has once seen it done? You loved your father,
and I could have loved him, for every word he spoke
in his trial was sweet and tolerant, but the weight
of what men are and have, rests heavy on
the graves of those who lost. They'll not rise again,
and their causes lie there with them.

Gaunt. If you mean to say
that Bartolomeo Romagna was innocent,
you are wrong. He was guilty.
There may have been injustice
from time to time, by regrettable chance, in our courts,
but not in that case, I assure you.

Mio. Oh, you assure me!
You lie in your scrag teeth, whoever you are!
My father was murdered!

Gaunt. Romagna was found guilty
by all due process of law, and given his chance
to prove his innocence.

Mio. What chance? When a court
panders to mob hysterics, and the jury
comes in loaded to soak an anarchist
and a foreigner, it may be due process of law
but it's also murder!

Gaunt. He should have thought of that
before he spilled blood.

Mio. He?

Gaunt. Sir, I know too well
that he was guilty.

Mio. Who are you? How do you know?
I've searched the records through, the trial and what
came after, and in all that million words
I found not one unbiased argument
to fix the crime on him.

Gaunt. And you yourself,
were you unprejudiced?

Mio. Who are you?

Esdras. Sir,
this gentleman is here, as you are here,
to ask my son, as you have asked, what ground
there might be for this talk of new evidence
in your father's case. We gave him the same answer
we've given you.

Mio. I'm sorry. I'd supposed
his cause forgotten except by myself. There's still
a defense committee then?

Gaunt. There may be. I
    am not connected with it.

Esdras. He is my guest,
    and asks to remain unknown.

Mio.

    [*After a pause, looking at Gaunt*]

    The judge at the trial
    was younger, but he had your face. Can it be
    that you're the man?—Yes—Yes.—The jury charge—
    I sat there as a child and heard your voice,
    and watched that Brahminical mouth. I knew even then
    you meant no good to him. And now you're here
    to winnow out truth and justice—the fountain-head
    of the lies that slew him! Are you Judge Gaunt?

Gaunt. I am.

Mio. Then tell me what damnation to what inferno
    would fit the toad that sat in robes and lied
    when he gave the charge, and knew he lied! Judge that,
    and then go to your place in that hell!

Gaunt. I know and have known
    what bitterness can rise against a court
    when it must say, putting aside all weakness,
    that a man's to die. I can forgive you that,
    for you are your father's son, and you think of him
    as a son thinks of his father. Certain laws
    seem cruel in their operation; it's necessary
    that we be cruel to uphold them. This cruelty
    is kindness to those I serve.

Mio. I don't doubt that.
    I know who it is you serve.

Gaunt. Would I have chosen
    to rack myself with other men's despairs,
    stop my ears, harden my heart, and listen only
    to the voice of law and light, if I had hoped
    some private gain for serving? In all my years
    on the bench of a long-established commonwealth
    not once has my decision been in question
    save in this case. Not once before or since.
    For hope of heaven or place on earth, or power
    or gold, no man has had my voice, nor will
    while I still keep the trust that's laid on me
    to sentence and define.

Mio. Then why are you here?

Gaunt. My record's clean. I've kept it so. But suppose
    with the best intent, among the myriad tongues
    that come to testify, I had missed my way
    and followed a perjured tale to a lethal end
    till a man was forsworn to death? Could I rest or sleep
    while there was doubt of this,
    even while there was question in a layman's mind?
    For always, night and day,
    there lies on my brain like a weight, the admonition:
    see truly, let nothing sway you; among all functions
    there's but one godlike, to judge. Then see to it
    you judge as a god would judge, with clarity,
    with truth, with what mercy is found consonant
    with order and law. Without law men are beasts,

and it's a judge's task to lift and hold them
above themselves. Let a judge be once mistaken
or step aside for a friend, and a gap is made
in the dykes that hold back anarchy and chaos,
and leave men bond but free.

Mio. Then the gap's been made,
and you made it.

Gaunt. I feared that too. May you be a judge
sometime, and know in what fear,
through what nights long
in fear, I scanned and verified and compared
the transcripts of the trial.

Mio. Without prejudice,
no doubt. It was never in your mind to prove
that you'd been right.

Gaunt. And conscious of that, too—
that that might be my purpose—watchful of that,
and jealous as his own lawyer of the rights
that should hedge the defendant!
And still I found no error,
shook not one staple of the bolts that linked
the doer to the deed! Still following on
from step to step, I watched all modern comment,
and saw it centered finally on one fact—
Garth Esdras was not called. This is Garth Esdras,
and you have heard him. Would his deposition
have justified a new trial?

Mio. No. It would not.

Gaunt. And there I come, myself. If the man were still
in his cell, and waiting, I'd have no faint excuse
for another hearing.

Mio. I've told you that I read
the trial from beginning to end. Every word you spoke
was balanced carefully to keep the letter
of the law and still convict—convict, by Christ,
if it tore the seven veils! You stand here now
running cascades of casuistry, to prove
to yourself and me that no judge of rank and breeding
could burn a man out of hate! But that's what you did
under all your varnish!

Gaunt. I've sought for evidence,
and you have sought. Have you found it? Can you cite
one fresh word in defence?

Mio. The trial itself
was shot full of legerdemain, prearranged to lead
the jury astray—

Gaunt. Could you prove that?

Mio. Yes!

Gaunt. And if
the jury were led astray, remember it's
the jury, by our Anglo-Saxon custom,
that finds for guilt or innocence. The judge
is powerless in that matter.

Mio. Not you! Your charge
misled the jury more than the evidence,
accepted every biased meaning, distilled
the poison for them!

Gaunt. But if that were so
   I'd be the first, I swear it, to step down
   among all men, and hold out both my hands
   for manacles—yes, publish it in the streets,
   that all I've held most sacred was defiled
   by my own act. A judge's brain becomes
   a delicate instrument to weigh men's lives
   for good and ill—too delicate to bear
   much tampering. If he should push aside
   the weights and throw the beam, and say, this once
   the man is guilty, and I will have it so
   though his mouth cry out from the ground,
   and all the world
   revoke my word, he'd have a short way to go
   to madness. I think you'd find him in the squares,
   stopping the passers-by with arguments,—
   see, I was right, the man was guilty there—
   this was brought in against him, this—and this—
   and I was left no choice! It's no light thing
   when a long life's been dedicate to one end
   to wrench the mind awry!

Mio. By your own thesis
   you should be mad, and no doubt you are.

Gaunt. But my madness
   is only this—that I would fain look back
   on a life well spent—without one stain—one breath
   of stain to flaw the glass—not in men's minds
   nor in my own. I take my God as witness
   I meant to earn that clearness, and believe
   that I have earned it. Yet my name is clouded

with the blackest, fiercest scandal of our age
that's touched a judge. What I can do to wipe
that smutch from my fame I will. I think you know
how deeply I've been hated, for no cause
that I can find there. Can it not be—and I ask this
quite honestly—that the great injustice lies
on your side and not mine? Time and time again
men have come before me perfect in their lives,
loved by all who knew them, loved at home,
gentle, not vicious, yet caught so ripe red-handed
in some dark violence there was no denying
where the onus lay.

Mio. That was not so with my father!

Gaunt. And yet it seemed so to me. To other men
who sat in judgment on him. Can you be sure—
I ask this in humility—that you,
who were touched closest by the tragedy,
may not have lost perspective—may have brooded
day and night on one theme—till your eyes are tranced
and show you one side only?

Mio. I see well enough.

Gaunt. And would that not be part of the malady—
to look quite steadily at the drift of things
but see there what you wish—not what is there—
not what another man to whom the story
was fresh would say is there?

Mio. You think I'm crazy.
Is that what you meant to say?

Gaunt. I've seen it happen
   with the best and wisest men. I but ask the question.
   I can't speak for you. Is it not true wherever
   you walk, through the little town where you knew him
     well,
   or flying from it, inland or by the sea,
   still walking at your side, and sleeping only
   when you too sleep, a shadow not your own
   follows, pleading and holding out its hands
   to be delivered from shame?

Mio. How you know that
   by God I don't know.

Gaunt. Because one spectre haunted you and me—
   and haunts you still, but for me it's laid to rest
   now that my mind is satisfied. He died
   justly and not by error.

   [*A pause*]

Mio.

   [*Stepping forward*]

   Do you care to know
   you've come so near to death it's miracle
   that pulse still beats in your splotchy throat?
   Do you know
   there's murder in me?

Gaunt. There was murder in your sire,
   and it's to be expected! I say he died
   justly, and he deserved it!

Mio. Yes, you'd like too well
 to have me kill you! That would prove your case
 and clear your name, and dip my father's name
 in stench forever! You'll not get that from me!
 Go home and die in bed, get it under cover,
 your lux-et-lex putrefaction of the right thing,
 you man that walks like a god!

Gaunt. Have I made you angry
 by coming too near the truth?

Mio. This sets him up,
 this venomous slug, this sets him up in a gown,
 deciding who's to walk above the earth
 and who's to lie beneath! And giving reasons!
 The cobra giving reasons; I'm a god,
 by Buddha, holy and worshipful my fang,
 and can I sink it in!

  [*He pauses, turns as if to go, then sits*]

 This is no good.
This won't help much.

  [*The* JUDGE *and* ESDRAS *look at each other*]

Gaunt. We should be going.

Esdras. Yes.

  [*They prepare to go*]

 I'll lend you my coat.
Gaunt.

  [*Looking at it with distaste*]

 No, keep it. A little rain
shouldn't matter to me.

Esdras. It freezes as it falls,
and you've a long way to go.

Gaunt. I'll manage, thank you.

> [GAUNT *and* ESDRAS *go out,* ESDRAS *obsequious, closing the door*]

Garth.

> [*Looking at Mio's back*]

Well?

Mio.

> [*Not moving*]

Let me sit here a moment.

> [GARTH *shrugs his shoulders and goes toward the inner door.* MIRIAMNE *opens it and comes out.* GARTH *looks at her, then at Mio, then lays his fingers on his lips. She nods.* GARTH *goes out.* MIRIAMNE *sits and watches* MIO. *After a little he turns and sees her*]

Mio. How did you come here?

Miriamne. I live here.

Mio. Here?

Miriamne. My name is Esdras. Garth
is my brother. The walls are thin.
I heard what was said.

Mio.

> [*Stirring wearily*]

I'm going. This is no place for me.

Miriamne. What place
would be better?

Mio. None. Only it's better to go.
Just to go.

> [*She comes over to him, puts her arm round him and kisses his
> forehead*]

Miriamne. Mio.

Mio. What do you want?
Your kisses burn me—and your arms. Don't offer
what I'm never to have! I can have nothing. They say
they'll cross the void sometime to the other planets
and men will breathe in that air.
Well, I could breathe there,
but not here now. Not on this ball of mud.
I don't want it.

Miriamne. They can take away so little
with all their words. For you're a king among them.
I heard you, and loved your voice.

Mio. I thought I'd fallen
so low there was no further, and now a pit
opens beneath. It was bad enough that he
should have died innocent, but if he were guilty—
then what's my life—what have I left to do—?
The son of a felon—and what they spat on me
was earned—and I'm drenched with the stuff.
Here on my hands
and cheeks, their spittle hanging! I liked my hands
because they were like his. I tell you I've lived

by his innocence, lived to see it flash
and blind them all—

Miriamne. Never believe them, Mio,
never.

[*She looks toward the inner door*]

Mio. But it was truth I wanted, truth—
not the lies you'd tell yourself, or tell a woman,
or a woman tells you! The judge with his cobra mouth
may have spat truth—and I may be mad! For me—
your hands are too clean to touch me. I'm to have
the scraps from hotel kitchens—and instead of love
those mottled bodies that hitch themselves through alleys
to sell for dimes or nickels. Go, keep yourself chaste
for the baker bridegroom—baker and son of a baker,
let him get his baker's dozen on you!

Miriamne. No—
say once you love me—say it once; I'll never
ask to hear it twice, nor for any kindness,
and you shall take all I have!

[GARTH *opens the inner door and comes out*]

Garth. I interrupt
a love scene, I believe. We can do without
your adolescent mawkishness.

[*To Miriamne*]

You're a child.
You'll both remember that.

Miriamne. I've said nothing to harm you—
and will say nothing.

Garth. You're my sister, though,
and I take a certain interest in you. Where
have you two met?

Miriamne. We danced together.

Garth. Then
the dance is over, I think.

Miriamne. I've always loved you
and tried to help you, Garth. And you've been kind.
Don't spoil it now.

Garth. Spoil it how?

Miriamne. Because I love him.
I didn't know it would happen. We danced together.
And the world's all changed. I see you through a mist,
and our father, too. If you brought this to nothing
I'd want to die.

Garth.

   [*To Mio*]

You'd better go.

Mio. Yes, I know.

   [*He rises. There is a trembling knock at the door.* MIRIAMNE
     goes to it. The HOBO *is there shivering*]

Hobo. Miss, could I sleep under the pipes tonight, miss?
Could I, please?

Miriamne. I think—not tonight.

Hobo. There won't be any more nights—
if I don't get warm, miss.

Miriamne. Come in.

> [*The* HOBO *comes in, looks round deprecatingly, then goes to a corner beneath a huge heating pipe, which he crawls under as if he'd been there before*]

Hobo. Yes, miss, thank you.

Garth. Must we put up with that?

Miriamne. Father let him sleep there—
last winter.

Garth. Yes, God, yes.

Mio. Well, good night.

Miriamne. Where will you go?

Mio. Yes, where? As if it mattered.

Garth. Oh, sleep here, too.
We'll have a row of you under the pipes.

Mio. No, thanks.

Miriamne. Mio, I've saved a little money. It's only
some pennies, but you must take it.

> [*She shakes some coins out of a box into her hand*]

Mio. No, thanks.

Miriamne. And I love you.
You've never said you love me.

Mio. Why wouldn't I love you
when you're clean and sweet,
and I've seen nothing sweet or clean

this last ten years? I love you. I leave you that
for what good it may do you. It's none to me.

Miriamne. Then kiss me.

Mio.

[*Looking at Garth*]

With that scowling over us? No.
When it rains, some spring
on the planet Mercury, where the spring comes often,
I'll meet you there, let's say. We'll wait for that.
It may be some time till then.

[*The outside door opens and* ESDRAS *enters with* JUDGE GAUNT,
then, after a slight interval, TROCK *follows.* TROCK
*surveys the interior and its occupants one by one, care-
fully*]

Trock. I wouldn't want to cause you inconvenience,
any of you, and especially the Judge.
I think you know that. You've all got things to do—
trains to catch, and so on. But trains can wait.
Hell, nearly anything can wait, you'll find,
only I can't. I'm the only one that can't
because I've got no time. Who's all this here?
Who's that?

[*He points to the Hobo*]

Esdras. He's a poor half-wit, sir,
that sometimes sleeps there.

Trock. Come out. I say come out,
whoever you are.

[*The* HOBO *stirs and looks up*]

Yes, I mean you. Come out.

[*The* HOBO *emerges*]

What's your name?

Hobo. They mostly call me Oke.

Trock. What do you know?

Hobo. No, sir.

Trock. Where are you from?

Hobo. I got a piece of bread.

[*He brings it out, trembling*]

Trock. Get back in there!

[*The* HOBO *crawls back into his corner*]

Maybe you want to know why I'm doing this.
Well, I've been robbed, that's why—
robbed five or six times;
the police can't find a thing—so I'm out for myself—
if you want to know.

[*To Mio*]

Who are you?

Mio. Oh, I'm a half-wit,
came in here by mistake. The difference is
I've got no piece of bread.

Trock. What's your name?

Mio. My name?
Theophrastus Such. That's respectable.
You'll find it all the way from here to the coast

on the best police blotters.
Only the truth is we're a little touched in the head,
Oke and me. You'd better ask somebody else.

Trock. Who is he?

Esdras. His name's Romagna. He's the son.

Trock. Then what's he doing here? You said you were on the level.

Garth. He just walked in. On account of the stuff in the papers. We didn't ask him.

Trock. God, we are a gathering. Now if we had Shadow we'd be all here, huh? Only I guess we won't see Shadow. No, that's too much to ask.

Mio. Who's Shadow?

Trock. Now you're putting questions. Shadow was just nobody, you see. He blew away. It might happen to anyone.

[*He looks at Garth*]

Yes, anyone at all.

Mio. Why do you keep your hand in your pocket, friend?

Trock. Because I'm cold, punk. Because I've been outside and it's cold as the tomb of Christ.

[*To Garth*]

Listen, there's a car waiting up at the street to take the Judge home. We'll take him to the car.

Garth. That's not necessary.

Esdras. No.

Trock. I say it is, see? You wouldn't want to let the Judge
   walk, would you? The Judge is going to ride where he's
   going, with a couple of chauffeurs, and everything done
   in style. Don't you worry about the Judge. He'll be
   taken care of. For good.

Garth. I want no hand in it.

Trock. Anything happens to me happens to you too,
   musician.

Garth. I know that.

Trock. Keep your mouth out of it then. And you'd better
   keep the punk here tonight, just for luck.

> [*He turns toward the door. There is a brilliant lightning flash
>   through the windows, followed slowly by dying thunder.*
>   TROCK *opens the door. The rain begins to pour in sheets*]

Jesus, somebody tipped it over again!

> [*A cough racks him*]

Wait till it's over. It takes ten days off me every time
   I step into it.

> [*He closes the door*]

Sit down and wait.

> [*Lightning flashes again. The thunder is fainter.* ESDRAS,
>   GARTH *and the* JUDGE *sit down*]

Gaunt. We were born too early. Even you who are young
   are not of the elect. In a hundred years
   man will put his finger on life itself, and then
   he will live as long as he likes. For you and me

we shall die soon—one day, one year more or less,
when or where, it's no matter. It's what we call
an indeterminate sentence. I'm hungry.

[GARTH *looks at Miriamne*]

Miriamne. There was nothing left
tonight.

Hobo. I've got a piece of bread.

[*He breaks his bread in two and hands half to the Judge*]

Gaunt. I thank you, sir.

[*He eats*]

This is not good bread.

[*He rises*]

Sir, I am used
to other company. Not better, perhaps, but their clothes
were different. These are what it's the fashion to call
the underprivileged.

Trock. Oh, hell!

[*He turns toward the door*]

Mio.

[*To Trock*]

It would seem that you and the Judge know each other.

[TROCK *faces him*]

Trock. I've been around.

Mio. Maybe you've met before.

Trock. Maybe we have.

Mio. Will you tell me where?

Trock. How long do you want to live?

Mio. How long? Oh, I've got big ideas about that.

Trock. I thought so. Well, so far I've got nothing against
you but your name, see? You keep it that way.

> [*He opens the door. The rain still falls in torrents. He closes the
> door. As he turns from it, it opens again, and* SHADOW,
> *white, bloodstained and dripping, stands in the doorway.*
> GARTH *rises.* TROCK *turns*]

Gaunt.

> [*To the Hobo*]

Yet if one were careful of his health, ate sparingly, drank
not at all, used himself wisely, it might be that even an
old man could live to touch immortality. They may
come on the secret sooner than we dare hope. You see?
It does no harm to try.

Trock.

> [*Backing away from Shadow*]

By God, he's out of his grave!

Shadow.

> [*Leaning against the doorway, holding a gun in his hands*

Keep your hands where they belong, Trock.
You know me.

Trock. Don't! Don't! I had nothing to do with it!

> [*He backs to the opposite wall*]

Shadow. You said the doctor gave you six months to live—
well, I don't give you that much. That's what you had,
six months, and so you start bumping off your friends
to make sure of your damn six months. I got it from you.
I know where I got it.
Because I wouldn't give it to the Judge.
So he wouldn't talk.

Trock. Honest to God—

Shadow. What God?
The one that let you put three holes in me
when I was your friend? Well, He let me get up again
and walk till I could find you. That's as far as I get,
but I got there, by God! And I can hear you
even if I can't see!

   [*He takes a staggering step forward*]

   A man needs blood
to keep going.—I got this far.—And now I can't see!
It runs out too fast—too fast—
when you've got three slugs
clean through you.
Show me where he is, you fools! He's here!
I got here!

   [*He drops the gun*]

   Help me! Help me! Oh, God! Oh, God!
I'm going to die! Where does a man lie down?
I want to lie down!

   [MIRIAMNE *starts toward Shadow.* GARTH *and* ESDRAS *help
      him into the next room,* MIRIAMNE *following.* TROCK
      squats in his corner, breathing hard, looking at the door.

Mio *stands, watching Trock.* Garth *returns, wiping his hand with a handkerchief.* Mio *picks up and pockets the gun.* Miriamne *comes back and leans against the door jamb*]

Gaunt. You will hear it said that an old man makes a good judge, being calm, clear-eyed, without passion. But this is not true. Only the young love truth and justice. The old are savage, wary, violent, swayed by maniac desires, cynical of friendship or love, open to bribery and the temptations of lust, corrupt and dastardly to the heart. I know these old men. What have they left to believe, what have they left to lose? Whorers of daughters, lickers of girls' shoes, contrivers of nastiness in the night, purveyors of perversion, worshippers of possession! Death is the only radical. He comes late, but he comes at last to put away the old men and give the young their places. It was time.

[*He leers*]

Here's one I heard yesterday:
>   Marmaduke behind the barn
>   got his sister in a fix;
>   he says damn instead of darn;
>   ain't he cute? He's only six!

The Hobo. He, he, he!

Gaunt.
>   And the hoot-owl hoots all night,
>   and the cuckoo cooks all day,
>   and what with a minimum grace of God
>   we pass the time away

The Hobo. He, he, he—I got ya!

[*He makes a sign with his thumb*]

Gaunt.

[*Sings*]

> And he led her all around
> and he laid her on the ground
> and he ruffled up the feathers of her
>   cuckoo's nest!

Hobo. Ho, ho, ho!

Gaunt. I am not taken with the way you laugh. You should cultivate restraint.

[ESDRAS *reënters*]

Trock. Shut the door.

Esdras. He won't come back again.

Trock. I want the door shut! He was dead, I tell you!

[*Esdras closes the door*]

And Romagna was dead, too, once! Can't they keep a man under ground?

Mio. No. No more! They don't stay under ground any more, and they don't stay under water! Why did you have him killed?

Trock. Stay away from me! I know you!

Mio. Who am I, then?

Trock. I know you, damn you! Your name's Romagna!

Mio. Yes! And Romagna was dead, too, and Shadow was dead, but the time's come when you can't keep them down, these dead men! They won't stay down! They come in with their heads shot off and their entrails dragging! Hundreds of them! One by one—all you ever had killed! Watch the door! See!—It moves!

Trock.

[*Looking, fascinated, at the door*]

Let me out of here!

[*He tries to rise*]

Mio.

[*The gun in his hand*]

Oh, no! You'll sit there and wait for them! One by one they'll come through that door, pulling their heads out of the gunny-sacks where you tied them—glauming over you with their rotten hands! They'll see without eyes and crawl over you—Shadow and the paymaster and all the rest of them—putrescent bones without eyes! Now! Look! Look! For I'm first among them!

Trock. I've done for better men than you! And I'll do for you!

Gaunt.

[*Rapping on the table*]

Order, gentlemen, order! The witness will remember that a certain decorum is essential in the court-room!

Mio. By God, he'll answer me!

Gaunt.

> [*Thundering*]

> Silence! Silence! Let me remind you of courtesy toward
> the witness! What case is this you try?

Mio. The case of the state against Bartolomeo Romagna
for the murder of the paymaster!

Gaunt. Sir, that was disposed of long ago!

Mio. Never disposed of, never, not while I live!

Gaunt. Then we'll have done with it now! I deny the
appeal! I have denied the appeal before and I do so
again!

Hobo. He, he!—He thinks he's in the moving pictures!

> [*A flash of lightning*]

Gaunt. Who set that flash! Bailiff, clear the court! This is
not Flemington, gentlemen! We are not conducting this
case to make a journalistic holiday!

> [*The thunder rumbles faintly.* GARTH *opens the outside door
> and faces a solid wall of rain*]

> Stop that man! He's one of the defendants!

> [GARTH *closes the door*]

Mio. Then put him on the stand!

Garth. What do you think you're doing?

Mio. Have you any objection?

Gaunt. The objection is not sustained. We will hear the
new evidence. Call your witness.

Mio. Garth Esdras!

Gaunt. He will take the stand!

Garth. If you want me to say what I said before I'll say it!

Mio. Call Trock Estrella then!

Gaunt. Trock Estrella to the stand!

Trock. No, by God!

Mio. Call Shadow, then! He'll talk! You thought he was
    dead, but he'll get up again and talk!

Trock.

    [*Screaming*]

    What do you want of me?

Mio. You killed the paymaster! You!

Trock. You lie! It was Shadow killed him!

Mio. And now I know! Now I know!

Gaunt. Again I remind you of courtesy toward the witness!

Mio. I know them now!
    Let me remind you of courtesy toward the dead!
    He says that Shadow killed him! If Shadow were here
    he'd say it was Trock! There were three men involved
    in the new version of the crime for which
    my father died! Shadow and Trock Estrella
    as principals in the murder—Garth as witness!—
    Why are they here together?—and you—the Judge—
    why are you here? Why, because you were all afraid

and you drew together out of that fear to arrange
a story you could tell! And Trock killed Shadow
and meant to kill the Judge out of that same fear—
to keep them quiet! This is the thing I've hunted
over the earth to find out, and I'd be blind
indeed if I missed it now!

   [To Gaunt]

  You heard what he said:
It was Shadow killed him! Now let the night conspire
with the sperm of hell! It's plain beyond denial
even to this fox of justice—and all his words
are curses on the wind! You lied! You lied!
You knew this too!

Gaunt.

   [Low]

  Let me go. Let me go!

Mio. Then why
  did you let my father die?

Gaunt. Suppose it known,
  but there are things a judge must not believe
  though they should head and fester underneath
  and press in on his brain. Justice once rendered
  in a clear burst of anger, righteously,
  upon a very common laborer,
  confessed an anarchist, the verdict found
  and the precise machinery of law
  invoked to know him guilty—think what furor
  would rock the state if the court then flatly said;

all this was lies—must be reversed? It's better,
as any judge can tell you, in such cases,
holding the common good to be worth more
than small injustice, to let the record stand,
let one man die. For justice, in the main,
is governed by opinion. Communities
will have what they will have, and it's quite as well,
after all, to be rid of anarchists. Our rights
as citizens can be maintained as rights
only while we are held to be the peers
of those who live about us. A vendor of fish
is not protected as a man might be
who kept a market. I own I've sometimes wished
this was not so, but it is. The man you defend
was unfortunate—and his misfortune bore
almost as heavily on me.—I'm broken—
broken across. You're much too young to know
how bitter it is when a worn connection chars
and you can't remember—can't remember.

   [*He steps forward*]

   You
will not repeat this? It will go no further?

Mio. No.
No further than the moon takes the tides—no further
than the news went when he died—
when you found him guilty
and they flashed that round the earth. Wherever men
still breathe and think, and know what's done to them
by the powers above, they'll know. That's all I ask.
That'll be enough.

[TROCK *has risen and looks darkly at Mio*]

Gaunt. Thank you. For I've said some things
a judge should never say.

Trock. Go right on talking.
Both of you. It won't get far, I guess.

Mio. Oh, you'll see to that?

Trock. I'll see to it. Me and some others.
Maybe I lost my grip there just for a minute.
That's all right.

Mio. Then see to it! Let it rain!
What can you do to me now when the night's on fire
with this thing I know? Now I could almost wish
there was a god somewhere—I could almost think
there was a god—and he somehow brought me here
and set you down before me here in the rain
where I could wring this out of you! For it's said,
and I've heard it, and I'm free! He was as I thought him,
true and noble and upright, even when he went
to a death contrived because he was as he was
and not your kind! Let it rain! Let the night speak fire
and the city go out with the tide, for he was a man
and I know you now, and I have my day!

> [*There is a heavy knock at the outside door*. MIRIAMNE *opens
> it, at a glance from* GARTH. *The* POLICEMAN *is there in
> oilskins*]

Policeman. Evening.

> [*He steps in, followed by a* SERGEANT, *similarly dressed*]

We're looking for someone
might be here. Seen an old man around
acting a little off?

[*To Esdras*]

You know the one
I mean. You saw him out there. Jeez! You've got
a funny crowd here!

[*He looks round. The* HOBO *shrinks into his corner*]

That's the one I saw.
What do you think?

Sergeant. That's him. You mean to say
you didn't know him by his pictures?

[*He goes to Gaunt*]

Come on, old man.
You're going home.

Gaunt. Yes, sir. I've lost my way.
I think I've lost my way.

Sergeant. I'll say you have.
About three hundred miles. Now don't you worry.
We'll get you back.

Gaunt. I'm a person of some rank
in my own city.

Sergeant. We know that. One look at you
and we'd know that.

Gaunt. Yes, sir.

Policeman. If it isn't Trock!
Trock Estrella. How are you, Trock?

Trock. Pretty good,
Thanks.

Policeman. Got out yesterday again, I hear?

Trock. That's right.

Sergeant. Hi'ye, Trock?

Trock. O.K.

Sergeant. You know we got orders
to watch you pretty close. Be good now, baby,
or back you go. Don't try to pull anything,
not in my district.

Trock. No, sir.

Sergeant. No bumping off.
If you want my advice quit carrying a gun.
Try earning your living for once.

Trock. Yeah.

Sergeant. That's an idea.
Because if we find any stiffs on the river bank
we'll know who to look for.

Mio. Then look in the other room!
I accuse that man of murder! Trock Estrella!
He's a murderer!

Policeman. Hello. I remember you.

Sergeant. Well, what murder?

Mio. It was Trock Estrella
  that robbed the pay roll thirteen years ago
  and did the killing my father died for! You know
  the Romagna case! Romagna was innocent,
  and Trock Estrella guilty!

Sergeant.

  [*Disgusted*]

  Oh, what the hell!
  That's old stuff—the Romagna case.

Policeman. Hey, Sarge!

  [*The* SERGEANT *and* POLICEMAN *come closer together*]

  The boy's a professional kidder. He took me over
  about half an hour ago. He kids the police
  and then ducks out!

Sergeant. Oh, yeah?

Mio. I'm not kidding now.
  You'll find a dead man there in the next room
  and Estrella killed him!

Sergeant. Thirteen years ago?
  And nobody smelled him yet?

Mio.

  [*Pointing*]

  I accuse this man
  of two murders! He killed the paymaster long ago
  and had Shadow killed tonight. Look, look for yourself!
  He's there all right!

Policeman. Look boy. You stood out there
  and put the booby sign on the dumb police
  because they're fresh out of Ireland. Don't try it twice.

Sergeant.

  [*To Garth*]

  Any corpses here?

Garth. Not that I know of.

Sergeant. I thought so.

  [Mɪo *looks at Miriamne*]
  [*To Mio*]

  Think up a better one.

Mio. Have I got to drag him
  out here where you can see him?

  [*He goes toward the inner door*]

  Can't you scent a murder
  when it's under your nose? Look in!

Miriamne. No, no—there's no one—there's no one there!

Sergeant.

  [*Looking at Miriamne*]

  Take a look inside.

Policeman. Yes, sir.

  [*He goes into the inside room. The* Sergeant *goes up to the
    door. The* Policeman *returns*]

  He's kidding, Sarge. If there's a cadaver
  in here I don't see it.

Mio. You're blind then!

    [*He goes into the room, the* SERGEANT *following him*]

Sergeant. What do you mean?

    [*He comes out,* MIO *following him*]

When you make a charge of murder it's better to have
the corpus delicti, son. You're the kind puts in
fire alarms to see the engine!

Mio. By God, he was there!
He went in there to die.

Sergeant. I'll bet he did.
And I'm Haile Selassie's aunt! What's your name?

Mio. Romagna.

    [*To Garth*]

What have you done with him?

Garth. I don't know what you mean.

Sergeant.

    [*To Garth*]

What's he talking about?

Garth. I wish I could tell you.
I don't know.

Sergeant. He must have seen something.

Policeman. He's got
the Romagna case on the brain. You watch yourself,
chump, or you'll get run in.

Mio. Then they're in it together!
All of them!

    [*To Miriamne*]

    Yes, and you!

Garth. He's nuts, I say.

Miriamne.

    [*Gently*]

You have dreamed something—isn't it true?
You've dreamed—
But truly, there was no one—

    [Mio *looks at her comprehendingly*]

Mio. You want me to say it.

    [*He pauses*]

Yes, by God, I was dreaming.

Sergeant.

    [*To Policeman*]

I guess you're right.
We'd better be going. Haven't you got a coat?

Gaunt. No, sir.

Sergeant. I guess I'll have to lend you mine.

    [*He puts his oilskins on Gaunt*]

Come on, now. It's getting late.

    [Gaunt, *the* Policeman *and the* Sergeant *go out*]

Trock. They're welcome to him.
His fuse is damp. Where is that walking fool
with the three slugs in him?

Esdras. He fell in the hall beyond
and we left him there.

Trock. That's lucky for some of us. Is he out this time
or is he still butting around?

Esdras. He's dead.

Trock. That's perfect.

   [*To Mio*]

   Don't try using your firearms, amigo baby,
the Sarge is outside.

   [*He turns to go*]

   Better ship that carrion
back in the river! The one that walks when he's dead;
maybe he'll walk the distance for you.

Garth. Coming back?

Trock. Well, if I come back,
you'll see me. If I don't, you won't. Let the punk
go far as he likes. Turn him loose and let him go.
And may you all rot in hell.

   [*He pulls his coat around him and goes to the left.* MIRIAMNE
     climbs up to look out a window]

Miriamne. He's climbing up to the street,
along the bridgehead.

   [*She turns*]

   Quick, Mio! It's safe now! Quick!

Garth. Let him do as he likes.

Miriamne. What do you mean? Garth! He means to kill
him!
You know that!

Garth. I've no doubt Master Romagna
can run his own campaign.

Miriamne. But he'll be killed!

Mio. Why did you lie about Shadow?

> [*There is a pause.* GARTH *shrugs, walks across the room, and
> sits*]

You were one of the gang!

Garth. I can take a death if I have to! Go tell your story,
only watch your step, for I warn you, Trock's out gunning
and you may not walk very far. Oh, I could defend it
but it's hardly worth while.
If they get Trock they get me too.
Go tell them. You owe me nothing.

Esdras. This Trock you saw,
no one defends him. He's earned his death so often
there's nobody to regret it. But his crime,
his same crime that has dogged you, dogged us down
from what little we had, to live here among the drains,
where the waterbugs break out like a scrofula
on what we eat—and if there's lower to go
we'll go there when you've told your story. And more
that I haven't heart to speak—

Mio.

> [*To Garth*]

My father died

in your place. And you could have saved him!
You were one of the gang!

Garth. Why, there you are.
   You certainly owe me nothing.

Miriamne.

   [*Moaning*]

   I want to die.
   I want to go away.

Mio. Yes, and you lied!
   And trapped me into it!

Miriamne. But Mio, he's my brother.
   I couldn't give them my brother.

Mio. No. You couldn't.
   You were quite right. The gods were damned ironic
   tonight, and they've worked it out.

Esdras. What will be changed
   if it comes to trial again? More blood poured out
   to a mythical justice, but your father lying still
   where he lies now.

Mio. The bright, ironical gods!
   What fun they have in heaven! When a man prays hard
   for any gift, they give it, and then one more
   to boot that makes it useless.

   [*To Miriamne*]

      You might have picked
   some other stranger to dance with!

Miriamne. I know.

Mio. Or chosen
some other evening to sit outside in the rain.
But no, it had to be this. All my life long
I've wanted only one thing, to say to the world
and prove it: the man you killed was clean and true
and full of love as the twelve-year-old that stood
and taught in the temple. I can say that now
and give my proofs—and now you stick a girl's face
between me and the rites I've sworn the dead
shall have of me! You ask too much! Your brother
can take his chance! He was ready enough to let
an innocent man take certainty for him
to pay for the years he's had. That parts us, then,
but we're parted anyway, by the same dark wind
that blew us together. I shall say what I have to say.

[*He steps back*]

And I'm not welcome here.

Miriamne. But don't go now! You've stayed
too long! He'll be waiting!

Mio. Well, is this any safer?
Let the winds blow, the four winds of the world,
and take us to the four winds.

[*The three are silent before him. He turns and goes out*]

CURTAIN

WINTERSET
ACT THREE

ACT THREE

SCENE: *The river bank outside the tenement, a little before the close of the previous act. The rain still falls through the street lamps. The* TWO NATTY YOUNG MEN IN SERGE AND GRAY *are leaning against the masonry in a ray of light, concentrating on a game of chance. Each holds in his hand a packet of ten or fifteen crisp bills. They compare the numbers on the top notes and immediately a bill changes hands. This goes on with varying fortune until the tide begins to run toward the* IST GUNMAN, *who has accumulated nearly the whole supply. They play on in complete silence, evidently not wishing to make any noise. Occasionally they raise their heads slightly to look carefully about. Luck begins to favor the* 2ND GUNMAN, *and the notes come his way. Neither evinces the slightest interest in how the game goes. They merely play on, bored, half-absorbed. There is a slight noise at the tenement door. They put the bills away and watch.* TROCK *comes out, pulls the door shut and comes over to them. He says a few words too low to be heard, and without changing expression the* YOUNG MEN *saunter toward the right.* TROCK *goes out to the left, and the* 2ND PLAYER, *catching that out of the corner of his eye, lingers in a glimmer of light to go on with the game. The* IST, *with an eye on the tenement door, begins to play without ado, and the bills again shift back and forth, then concentrate in the hands of the* IST GUNMAN. *The* 2ND *shrugs his shoulders, searches his pockets, finds one bill, and playing with it begins to win heavily. They hear the door opening, and putting the notes away, slip out in front of the rock.* MIO *emerges, closes the door, looks round him and walks to the left. Near the corner of the tenement he pauses, reaches out his hand to try the rain, looks up toward the street, and stands uncertainly a moment. He returns and leans against the tenement wall.* MIRIAMNE *comes out.* MIO *continues to look off into space as if unaware of her. She looks away.*

Mio. This rather takes one off his high horse.—What I

113

mean, tough weather for a hegira. You see, this is my sleeping suit, and if I get it wet—basta!

Miriamne. If you could only hide here.

Mio. Hide?

Miriamne. Lucia would take you in. The street-piano man.

Mio. At the moment I'm afflicted with claustrophobia. I prefer to die in the open, seeking air.

Miriamne. But you could stay there till daylight.

Mio. You're concerned about me.

Miriamne. Shall I ask him?

Mio. No. On the other hand there's a certain reason in your concern. I looked up the street and our old friend Trock hunches patiently under the warehouse eaves.

Miriamne. I was sure of that.

Mio. And here I am, a young man on a cold night, waiting the end of the rain. Being read my lesson by a boy, a blind boy—you know the one I mean. Knee-deep in the salt-marsh, Miriamne, bitten from within, fought.

Miriamne. Wouldn't it be better if you came back in the house?

Mio. You forget my claustrophobia.

Miriamne. Let me walk with you, then. Please. If I stay beside you he wouldn't dare.

Mio. And then again he might.—We don't speak the same language, Miriamne.

Miriamne. I betrayed you. Forgive me.

Mio. I wish I knew this region. There's probably a path along the bank.

Miriamne. Yes. Shadow went that way.

Mio. That's true, too. So here I am, a young man on a wet night, and blind in my weather eye. Stay and talk to me.

Miriamne. If it happens—it's my fault.

Mio. Not at all, sweet. You warned me to keep away. But I would have it. Now I have to find a way out. It's like a chess game. If you think long enough there's always a way out.—For one or the other.—I wonder why white always wins and black always loses in the problems. White to move and mate in three moves. But what if white were to lose—ah, what then? Why, in that case, obviously black would be white and white would be black.—As it often is.—As we often are.—Might makes white. Losers turn black. Do you think I'd have time to draw a gun?

Miriamne. No.

Mio. I'm a fair shot. Also I'm fair game.

> [*The door of the tenement opens and* GARTH *comes out to look about quickly. Seeing only Mio and Miriamne he goes in and comes out again almost immediately carrying one end of a door on which a body lies covered with a cloth. The* HOBO *carries the other end. They go out to the right with their burden*]

This is the burial of Shadow, then;
feet first he dips, and leaves the haunts of men.

Let us make mourn for Shadow, wetly lying,
in elegiac stanzas and sweet crying.
Be gentle with him, little cold waves and fishes;
nibble him not, respect his skin and tissues—

Miriamne. Must you say such things?

Mio. My dear, some requiem is fitting over the dead, even
for Shadow. But the last rhyme was bad.

Whittle him not, respect his dying wishes.

That's better. And then to conclude:

His aromatic virtues, slowly rising
will circumnamb the isle, beyond disguising.
He clung to life beyond the wont of men.
Time and his silence drink us all. Amen.

How I hate these identicals. The French allow them, but
the French have no principles anyway. You know, Miriamne, there's really nothing mysterious about human
life. It's purely mechanical, like an electric appliance.
Stop the engine that runs the generator and the current's
broken. When we think the brain gives off a small electric discharge—quite measurable, and constant within
limits. But that's not what makes your hair stand up
when frightened.

Miriamne. I think it's a mystery.

Mio. Human life? We'll have to wear veils if we're to keep
it a mystery much longer. Now if Shadow and I were
made up into sausages we'd probably make very good
sausages.

Miriamne. Don't—

Mio. I'm sorry. I speak from a high place, far off, long ago, looking down. The cortège returns.

[GARTH *and the* HOBO *return, carrying the door, the cloth lying loosely over it*]

I hope you placed an obol in his mouth to pay the ferry-man? Even among the Greeks a little money was pre-requisite to Elysium.

[GARTH *and the* HOBO *go inside, silent*]

No? It's grim to think of Shadow lingering among lesser shades on the hither side. For lack of a small gratuity.

[ESDRAS *comes out the open door and closes it behind him*]

Esdras. You must wait here, Mio, or go inside. I know you don't trust me, and I haven't earned your trust. You're young enough to seek truth—
and there is no truth;
and I know that—
but I shall call the police and see that you
get safely off.

Mio. It's a little late for that.

Esdras. I shall try.

Mio. And your terms? For I daresay you make terms?

Esdras. No.

Mio. Then let me remind you what will happen.
The police will ask some questions.
When they're answered

they'll ask more, and before they're done with it
your son will be implicated.

Esdras. Must he be?

Mio. I shall not keep quiet.

   [*A pause*]

Esdras. Still, I'll go.

Mio. I don't ask help, remember. I make no truce.
He's not on my conscience, and I'm not on yours.

Esdras. But you
could make it easier, so easily.
He's my only son. Let him live.

Mio. His chance of survival's
better than mine, I'd say.

Esdras. I'll go.

Mio. I don't urge it.

Esdras. No. I put my son's life in your hands.
When you're gone,
that may come to your mind.

Mio. Don't count on it.

Esdras. Oh,
I count on nothing.

   [*He turns to go.* MIRIAMNE *runs over to him and silently
   kisses his hands*]

Not mine, not mine, my daughter!
They're guilty hands.

   [*He goes out left.* GARTH'S *violin is heard within*]

Mio. There was a war in heaven
once, all the angels on one side, and all
the devils on the other, and since that time
disputes have raged among the learned, concerning
whether the demons won, or the angels. Maybe
the angels won, after all.

Miriamne. And again, perhaps
there are no demons or angels.

Mio. Oh, there are none.
But I could love your father.

Miriamne. I love him. You see,
he's afraid because he's old. The less one has
to lose the more he's afraid.

Mio. Suppose one had
only a short stub end of life, or held
a flashlight with the batteries run down
till the bulb was dim, and knew that he could live
while the glow lasted. Or suppose one knew
that while he stood in a little shelter of time
under a bridgehead, say, he could live, and then,
from then on, nothing. Then to lie and turn
with the earth and sun, and regard them not in the least
when the bulb was extinguished or he stepped beyond
his circle into the cold? How would he live
that last dim quarter-hour, before he went,
minus all recollection, to grow in grass
between cobblestones?

Miriamne. Let me put my arms round you, Mio.
Then if anything comes, it's for me, too.

    [*She puts both arms round him*]

Mio. Only suppose
   this circle's charmed! To be safe until he steps
   from this lighted space into dark! Time pauses here
   and high eternity grows in one quarter-hour
   in which to live.

Miriamne. Let me see if anyone's there—
   there in the shadows.

   [*She looks toward the right*]

Mio. It might blast our eternity—
   blow it to bits. No, don't go. This is forever,
   here where we stand. And I ask you, Miriamne,
   how does one spend a forever?

Miriamne. You're frightened?

Mio. Yes.
   So much that time stands still.

Miriamne. Why didn't I speak—
   tell them—when the officers were here? I failed you
   in that one moment!

Mio. His life for mine? Oh, no.
   I wouldn't want it, and you couldn't give it.
   And if I should go on living we're cut apart
   by that brother of yours.

Miriamne. Are we?

Mio. Well, think about it.
   A body lies between us, buried in quicklime.
   Your allegiance is on the other side of that grave
   and not to me.

Miriamne. No, Mio! Mio, I love you!

Mio. I love you, too, but in case my life went on
beyond that barrier of dark—then Garth
would run his risk of dying.

Miriamne. He's punished, Mio.
His life's been torment to him. Let him go,
for my sake, Mio.

Mio. I wish I could. I wish
I'd never seen him—or you. I've steeped too long
in this thing. It's in my teeth and bones. I can't
let go or forget. And I'll not add my lie
to the lies that cumber his ground. We live our days
in a storm of lies that drifts the truth too deep
for path or shovel; but I've set my foot on a truth
for once, and I'll trail it down!

    [*A silence.* Miriamne *looks out to the right*]

Miriamne. There's someone there—
I heard—

    [Carr *comes in from the right*]

Mio. It's Carr.

Carr. That's right. No doubt about it.
Excuse me.

Mio. Glad to see you. This is Miriamne.
Carr's a friend of mine.

Carr. You're better employed
than when I saw you last.

Mio. Bow to the gentleman,
Miriamne. That's meant for you.

Miriamne. Thank you, I'm sure.
Should I leave you, Mio? You want to talk?

Mio. Oh, no,
we've done our talking.

Miriamne. But—

Carr. I'm the one's out of place—
I wandered back because I got worried about you,
that's the truth.—Oh—those two fellows with the hats
down this way, you know, the ones that ran
after we heard the shooting—they're back again,
lingering or malingering down the bank,
revisiting the crime, I guess. They may
mean well.

Mio. I'll try to avoid them.

Carr. I didn't care
for the way they looked at me.—No luck, I suppose,
with that case history? The investigation
you had on hand?

Mio. I can't say. By the way,
the stiff that fell in the water and we saw swirling
down the eddy, he came trudging up, later on,
long enough to tell his name. His name was Shadow,
but he's back in the water now. It's all in an evening.
These things happen here.

Carr. Good God!

Mio. I know.
I wouldn't believe it if you told it.

Carr. But—
the man was alive?

Mio. Oh, not for long! He's dunked
for good this time. That's all that's happened

Carr. Well,
if you don't need me—

Miriamne. You had a message to send—
have you forgotten—?

Mio. I?—Yes, I had a message—
but I won't send it—not now.

Miriamne. Then I will—!

Mio. No.
Let it go the way it is! It's all arranged
another way. You've been a good scout, Carr,
the best I ever knew on the road.

Carr. That sounds
like making your will.

Mio. Not yet, but when I do
I've thought of something to leave you. It's the view
of Mt. Rainier from the Seattle jail,
snow over cloud. And the rusty chain in my pocket
from a pair of handcuffs my father wore. That's all
the worldly goods I'm seized of.

Carr. Look, Mio—hell—
if you're in trouble—

Mio. I'm not. Not at all. I have
a genius that attends me where I go,
and guards me now. I'm fine.

Carr. Well, that's good news.
He'll have his work cut out.

Mio. Oh, he's a genius.

Carr. I'll see you then.
I'll be at the Grand Street place. I'm lucky tonight,
and I can pay. I could even pay for two.

Mio. Thanks, I may take you up.

Carr. Good night.

Mio. Right, Carr.

Carr.

   [*To Miriamne*]

Good night.

Miriamne.

   [*After a pause*]

Good night.

   [Carr *goes out to the left*]

Why did you do that? He's your genius, Mio,
and you let him go.

Mio. I couldn't help it.

Miriamne. Call him.
Run after him and call him!

Mio. I tried to say it
and it strangled in my throat. I might have known
you'd win in the end.

Miriamne. Is it for me?

Mio. For you?
It stuck in my throat, that's all I know.

Miriamne. Oh, Mio,
I never asked for that! I only hoped
Garth could go clear.

Mio. Well, now he will.

Miriamne. But you—
It was your chance!

Mio. I've lost
my taste for revenge if it falls on you. Oh, God,
deliver me from the body of this death
I've dragged behind me all these years! Miriamne!
Miriamne!

Miriamne. Yes!

Mio. Miriamne, if you love me
teach me a treason to what I am, and have been,
till I learn to live like a man! I think I'm waking
from a long trauma of hate and fear and death
that's hemmed me from my birth—and glimpse a life
to be lived in hope—but it's young in me yet, I can't
get free, or forgive! But teach me how to live
and forget to hate!

Miriamne. He would have forgiven.

Mio. He?

Miriamne. Your father.

> [*A pause*]

Mio. Yes.

> [*Another pause*]
> You'll think it strange, but I've never
> remembered that.

Miriamne. How can I help you?

Mio. You have.

Miriamne. If I were a little older—if I knew
the things to say! I can only put out my hands
and give you back the faith you bring to me
by being what you are. Because to me
you are all hope and beauty and brightness drawn
across what's black and mean!

Mio. He'd have forgiven—
Then there's no more to say—I've groped long enough
through this everglades of old revenges—here
the road ends.—Miriamne, Miriamne,
the iron I wore so long—it's eaten through
and fallen from me. Let me have your arms.
They'll say we're children—Well—the world's made up
of children.

Miriamne. Yes.

Mio. But it's too late for me.

Miriamne. No.

> [*She goes into his arms, and they kiss for the first time*]

Then we'll meet again?

Mio. Yes.

Miriamne. Where?

Mio. I'll write—
or send Carr to you.

Miriamne. You won't forget?

Mio. Forget?
Whatever streets I walk, you'll walk them, too,
from now on, and whatever roof or stars
I have to house me, you shall share my roof
and stars and morning. I shall not forget.

Miriamne. God keep you!

Mio. And keep you. And this to remember!
if I should die, Miriamne, this half-hour
is our eternity. I came here seeking
light in darkness, running from the dawn,
and stumbled on a morning.

> [*One of the* YOUNG MEN IN SERGE *strolls in casually from the
> right, looks up and down without expression, then,
> seemingly having forgotten something, retraces his steps
> and goes out.* ESDRAS *comes in slowly from the left.
> He has lost his hat, and his face is bleeding from a
> slight cut on the temple. He stands abjectly near the
> tenement*]

Miriamne. Father—what is it?

> [*She goes towards Esdras*]

Esdras. Let me alone.

> [*He goes nearer to Mio*]

He wouldn't let me pass.
The street's so icy up along the bridge
I had to crawl on my knees—he kicked me back
three times—and then he held me there—I swear
what I could do I did! I swear to you
I'd save you if I could.

Mio. What makes you think
that I need saving?

Esdras. Child, save yourself if you can!
He's waiting for you.

Mio. Well, we knew that before.

Esdras. He won't wait much longer. He'll come here—
he told me so. Those damned six months of his—
he wants them all—and you're to die—you'd spread
his guilt—I had to listen to it—

Mio. Wait—

[*He walks forward and looks casually to the right, then returns*]

There must be some way up through the house and out
across the roof—

Esdras. He's watching that. But come in—
and let me look.—

Mio. I'll stay here, thanks. Once in
and I'm a rat in a deadfall—I'll stay here—
look for me if you don't mind.

Esdras. Then watch for me—
I'll be on the roof—

[*He goes in hurriedly*]

Mio.

[*Looking up*]

Now all you silent powers
that make the sleet and dark, and never yet
have spoken, give us a sign, let the throw be ours
this once, on this longest night, when the winter sets
his foot on the threshold leading up to spring
and enters with remembered cold—let fall
some mercy with the rain. We are two lovers
here in your night, and we wish to live.

Miriamne. Oh, Mio—
if you pray that way, nothing good will come!
You're bitter, Mio.

Mio. How many floors has this building?

Miriamne. Five or six. It's not as high as the bridge.

Mio. No, I thought not. How many pomegranate seeds
did you eat, Persephone?

Miriamne. Oh, darling, darling,
if you die, don't die alone.

Mio. I'm afraid I'm damned
to hell, and you're not damned at all. Good God,
how long he takes to climb!

Miriamne. The stairs are steep.

[*A slight pause*]

Mio. I'll follow him.

Miriamne. He's there—at the window—now.
He waves you to go back, not to go in.

Mio, see, that path between the rocks—
they're not watching that—they're out at the river—
I can see them there—they can't watch both—
it leads to a street above.

Mio. I'll try it, then.
Kiss me. You'll hear. But if you never hear—
then I'm the king of hell, Persephone,
and I'll expect you.

Miriamne. Oh, lover, keep safe.

Mio. Good-bye.

> [*He slips out quickly between the rocks. There is a quick machine gun rat-tat. The violin stops.* MIRIAMNE *runs toward the path.* MIO *comes back slowly, a hand pressed under his heart*]

It seems you were mistaken.

Miriamne. Oh, God, forgive me!

> [*She puts an arm round him. He sinks to his knees*]

Where is it, Mio? Let me help you in! Quick, quick,
let me help you!

Mio. I hadn't thought to choose—this—ground—
but it will do.

> [*He slips down*]

Miriamne. Oh, God, forgive me!

Mio. Yes?
The king of hell was not forgiven then,
Dis is his name, and Hades is his home—
and he goes alone—

Miriamne. Why does he bleed so? Mio, if you go
  I shall go with you.

Mio. It's better to stay alive.
  I wanted to stay alive—because of you—
  I leave you that—and what he said to me dying:
  I love you, and will love you after I die.
  Tomorrow, I shall still love you, as I've loved
  the stars I'll never see, and all the mornings
  that might have been yours and mine. Oh, Miriamne,
  you taught me this.

Miriamne. If only I'd never seen you
  then you could live—

Mio. That's blasphemy—Oh, God,
  there might have been some easier way of it.
  You didn't want me to die, did you, Miriamne—?
  You didn't send me away—?

Miriamne. Oh, never, never—

Mio. Forgive me—kiss me—I've got blood on your lips—
  I'm sorry—it doesn't matter—I'm sorry—

   [ESDRAS *and* GARTH *come out*]

Miriamne. Mio—
  I'd have gone to die myself—you must hear this, Mio,
  I'd have died to help you—you must listen, sweet,
  you must hear it—

   [*She rises*]

   I can die, too, see! You! There!
  You in the shadows!—You killed him to silence him!

   [*She walks toward the path*]

But I'm not silenced! All that he knew I know,
and I'll tell it tonight! Tonight—
tell it and scream it
through all the streets—that Trock's a murderer
and he hired you for this murder!
Your work's not done—
and you won't live long! Do you hear?
You're murderers, and I know who you are!

[*The machine gun speaks again. She sinks to her knees.* GARTH
runs to her]

Garth. You little fool!

[*He tries to lift her*]

Miriamne. Don't touch me!

[*She crawls toward Mio*]

Look, Mio! They killed me, too. Oh, you can believe me
now, Mio. You can believe I wouldn't hurt you,
because I'm dying! Why doesn't he answer me?
Oh, now he'll never know!

[*She sinks down, her hand over her mouth, choking.* GARTH
kneels beside her, then rises, shuddering. The HOBO
comes out. LUCIA *and* PINY *look out*]

Esdras. It lacked only this.

Garth. Yes.

[ESDRAS *bends over Miriamne, then rises slowly*]

Why was the bastard born? Why did he come here?

Esdras. Miriamne—Miriamne—yes, and Mio,
one breath shall call you now—forgive us both—

forgive the ancient evil of the earth
that brought you here—

Garth. Why must she be a fool?

Esdras. Well, they were wiser than you and I. To die
when you are young and untouched, that's beggary
to a miser of years, but the devils locked in synod
shake and are daunted when men set their lives
at hazard for the heart's love, and lose. And these,
who were yet children, will weigh more than all
a city's elders when the experiment
is reckoned up in the end. Oh, Miriamne,
and Mio—Mio, my son—know this where you lie,
this is the glory of earth-born men and women,
not to cringe, never to yield, but standing,
take defeat implacable and defiant,
die unsubmitting. I wish that I'd died so,
long ago; before you're old you'll wish
that you had died as they have. On this star,
in this hard star-adventure, knowing not
what the fires mean to right and left, nor whether
a meaning was intended or presumed,
man can stand up, and look out blind, and say:
in all these turning lights I find no clue,
only a masterless night, and in my blood
no certain answer, yet is my mind my own,
yet is my heart a cry toward something dim
in distance, which is higher than I am
and makes me emperor of the endless dark
even in seeking! What odds and ends of life
men may live otherwise, let them live, and then

go out, as I shall go, and you. Our part
is only to bury them. Come, take her up.
They must not lie here.

[Lucia *and* Piny *come near to help.* Esdras *and* Garth *stoop*
to carry Miriamne]

CURTAIN